Supply Chain Management

DeMYSTiFieD®

DeMYSTiFieD® Series

Accounting Demystified
Advanced Calculus Demystified
Advanced Physics Demystified
Advanced Statistics Demystified
Algebra Demystified
Alternative Energy Demystified
Anatomy Demystified
Astronomy Demystified
Audio Demystified
Biology Demystified
Biotechnology Demystified
Business Calculus Demystified
Business Math Demystified
Business Statistics Demystified
C++ Demystified
Calculus Demystified
Chemistry Demystified
Chinese Demystified
Circuit Analysis Demystified
College Algebra Demystified
Corporate Finance Demystified
Databases Demystified
Data Structures Demystified
Differential Equations Demystified
Digital Electronics Demystified
Earth Science Demystified
Electrician's Trade Demystified
Electricity Demystified
Electronics Demystified
Engineering Statistics Demystified
Environmental Science Demystified
Ethics Demystified
Everyday Math Demystified
Fertility Demystified
Financial Planning Demystified
Forensics Demystified
French Demystified
Genetics Demystified
Geometry Demystified
German Demystified
Investing Demystified
Italian Demystified
Japanese Demystified
Java Demystified

JavaScript Demystified
Lean Six Sigma Demystified
Linear Algebra Demystified
Logic Demystified
Macroeconomics Demystified
Management Accounting Demystified
Math Proofs Demystified
Math Word Problems Demystified
MATLAB® Demystified
Medical Billing and Coding Demystified
Medical Terminology Demystified
Meteorology Demystified
Microbiology Demystified
Microeconomics Demystified
Nanotechnology Demystified
Nurse Management Demystified
OOP Demystified
Options Demystified
Organic Chemistry Demystified
Pharmacology Demystified
Philosophy Demystified
Physics Demystified
Physiology Demystified
Pre-Algebra Demystified
Precalculus Demystified
Probability Demystified
Project Management Demystified
Psychology Demystified
Quality Management Demystified
Quantum Mechanics Demystified
Real Estate Math Demystified
Relativity Demystified
Robotics Demystified
Sales Management Demystified
Signals and Systems Demystified
Six Sigma Demystified
Spanish Demystified
sql Demystified
Statics and Dynamics Demystified
Statistics Demystified
Supply Chain Management Demystified
Technical Analysis Demystified
Technical Math Demystified
Trigonometry Demystified

Supply Chain
Management
DeMYSTiFieD®

John M. McKeller

New York   Chicago   San Francisco   Athens   London   Madrid
Mexico City   Milan   New Delhi   Singapore   Sydney   Toronto

Supply Chain Management DeMYSTiFieD®

1 2 3 4 5 6 7 8 9 0   DOC/DOC   1 2 0 9 8 7 6 5 4

ISBN 978-0-07-180512-4
MHID 0-07-180512-5

Sponsoring Editor	Project Manager	Indexer
Judy Bass	Nancy Dimitry, D&P Editorial Services	WordCo Indexing Services
Editing Supervisor		**Cover Illustration**
Stephen M. Smith	**Copy Editor**	Lance Lekander
	Joe Cavanagh, D&P Editorial Services	
Production Supervisor		**Art Director, Cover**
Pamela A. Pelton	**Proofreader**	Jeff Weeks
Acquisitions Coordinator	Don Dimitry, D&P Editorial Services	**Composition**
Amy Stonebraker		D&P Editorial Services

About the Author

John M. McKeller is a senior lecturer in the Wisconsin School of Business at the University of Wisconsin—Madison (UW-Madison). He teaches undergraduate and graduate classes in supply management and global sourcing in the School's Grainger Center for Supply Chain Management. John previously served concurrent appointments as the director of education for the Institute for Supply Management and as an assistant professor at UW-Madison. He was also director of the supply chain management programs in UW-Madison's former executive education supply chain management certificate series.

John has been an adjunct faculty member at Arizona State University, the University of San Diego, and the University of California at San Diego. Before entering the academic field, he held various managerial positions with subsidiaries of major U.S. corporations. A graduate of San Diego State University, John also completed an MBA at Pepperdine University and a DBA at United States International University.

Contents

Preface

During the last twenty-five years, many brilliant academics, researchers, and practitioners have contributed to a growing body of knowledge about supply chain management. Several excellent textbooks and professional books are available that cover supply chain management in great depth and from varying perspectives, such as an emphasis on logistics, supply management, or operations. (Several of these are listed in the Appendix.)

This book is intended to fill the space between the frequently esoteric and theoretical perspectives of academic books and the detailed complexity of those often written for professionals. It was created specifically to help students who have had no exposure to supply-chain-related coursework or working professionals who need an understanding of fundamental supply chain concepts.

Given the assumptions above, the book's chapters bring a novice reader into supply chain management through a step-by-step process. This starts with the exploration and explanation of related topics and then builds upon that base. Each chapter was purposely written to focus on major elements of a specific topic that will ultimately provide the reader with a foundation of supply chain knowledge. For those who wish to read additional anecdotes and case scenarios not included in the chapters, several are provided in the Appendix.

In the preface to his classic textbook, *Designing and Managing the Supply Chain*, Professor David Simchi-Levi of MIT wrote:

> *Of course, supply chain management is a very broad area, and it would be impossible for a single book to cover all of the relevant areas in depth. Indeed, there is considerable disagreement in academia and industry about exactly what these relevant areas are.*

That realistic assessment for his exceptional work is even far more applicable to this modest book. After you finish reading it, you'll have a fundamental understanding of what supply chain management is, why it is important, and what the emerging practices in the field are. However, it is hoped that the basics you learn here will only stimulate your interest toward further study in this important, multifaceted, and dynamic discipline. A short list of some books and Internet resources are available in the Appendix for those who wish to continue their learning experience.

John M. McKeller

Acknowledgments

This book is a modest contribution to McGraw-Hill's excellent *Demystified* series, and it has been a privilege to write it. I greatly appreciate the knowledge and insights gained from many esteemed individuals whose scholarly work has been invaluable in shaping this author's understanding of supply chain management.

Beyond the brilliant writing of academics, researchers, and other professionals, the personal assistance provided by colleagues and family members deserves recognition. In the Wisconsin School of Business, Professor John (Jack) R. Nevin, Ph.D. and Faculty Associate Verda A. Blythe were always there to help with insights and support. My sister Michelle McAlea contributed her expertise in proofreading, my brother Joe with the graphics. My daughter Brianna's critiques of writing style were invaluable, and of course, my wife Irina's immeasurable patience with me is always an asset.

Very special thanks go to my long-time friend and mentor, Professor Richard L. Pinkerton, Ph.D., and my McGraw-Hill editor, Judy Bass. Their help was critical in so many ways that without them this book would never have happened.

Supply Chain Management

DeMYSTiFieD®

chapter 1

Basic Supply Chain Management Concepts

No enterprise can succeed by itself. Competing in a complex global business environment requires an interdependent network of many organizations. That's why excellence in *supply chain management* is critical for success. This chapter will explain what supply chain management is and review different perspectives on how to maximize its contribution to organizational success.

CHAPTER OBJECTIVES

In this chapter, you will learn

- What the terms *supply chain* and *supply chain management* mean.
- What *supply chain networks* are.
- What *demand chains* and *value chains* are.
- How customers determine value.
- How *service supply chains* differ from *product supply chains*.
- Why supply chain management has become a "hot topic."

Supply Chain and Supply Chain Management

We are all customers. Whether we shop in stores or online, everyone can identify with buying things. When people pick up a six-pack of their favorite beverage from a local grocery, do they know where it came from? It's easy to think, "It comes from the local supermarket." But the supermarket doesn't make it—retailers only provide a convenient location to stock and display a product until it is purchased. The store is just the last point in a long chain of supply that begins with the raw materials in the earth before it ends with us. Almost none of the products or services we purchase are the result of a single individual's or organization's efforts. Many suppliers, manufacturers, transporters, wholesalers, distributors, retailers, service professionals, trades people, and others contributed to providing that purchased product or service.

Supply chain is a metaphor used to represent all the individual firms, their personnel, and the physical infrastructure required to create and transport products to customers. Joined together by interconnected processes, supply chain members move materials, information, and money (finance) in response to customers' demands. Because supply chain management is a relatively new term, there are many definitions for it. Although different, they all have some common elements:

- Customer focus
- Value-adding processes
- Planning and management
- Integration and collaboration

The term supply chain management was first used to illustrate the need for a more comprehensive view of what it took to meet customer demands. The original idea was to help identify and eliminate waste and excess cost. What was also needed was a way to highlight the problems caused when internal organizational functions acted independently of each other. Supply chain management thinking brought organizations a new perspective based on a vision of an extended enterprise: a complex system that included suppliers, distributors, retailers, and other internal and external organizations.

The result of this vision was a concept that promotes collaboration between both the internal and external members in a chain of supply (or "supply chain"). It showed that a focus on any one internal element, such as logistics, was not an effective way to manage operations. Thus, meeting the need for integration and collaboration became a key aspect of supply chain management. Now, attention is paid to creating and sustaining it, while multiple value-adding processes are coordinated in an integrated system.

Supply chain management also had origins in some early initiatives that sought to reduce costs and improve efficiencies through what were then emerging technologies.

- In the 1980s, *quick response logistics* (QRL) strategies were developed in the apparel industry and then were adopted by general merchandise retailers along with *Universal Product Codes* (UPC) and *electronic data interchange* (EDI) processes.
- In the 1990s, the *efficient consumer response* (ECR) initiative was launched in the grocery industry. It further exploited UPC, EDI, and *point of sale* (POS) data-capturing technologies in order to improve demand management, scheduling, and inventory management. Also in the 1990s, *Collaborative Planning, Forecasting, and Replenishment* (CPFR) evolved from initiatives launched by companies such as Wal-Mart, Sears, and J. C. Penney.

As used in this text, supply chain management is the collaborative governance of all the elements in a system used to provide products and services to customers. This includes the integrative management of both internal processes across functional lines and external processes with suppliers and customers. Because there are some important differences between them, early supply chain definitions were manufacturing oriented and not immediately applied to services. That has changed, and the term is now often used to represent the systems required to furnish customers with either products or services.

Logistics and Supply Chain Management

The term *logistics* evolved from its use by the military in reference to the planning, movement, and storage of supplies to troops in the field. Essentially, it includes the processes required for the flow of goods from where they are produced to where they are used or consumed. Transportation, inventory management, and warehousing are considered part of the logistics function in a commercial enterprise.

Although they are brought together under the banner of logistics, these internal processes may still operate as separate, functionally aligned departments. This circumstance creates inefficiency because of conflicting objectives, disjointed performance metrics, and a lack of coordination and communication. A

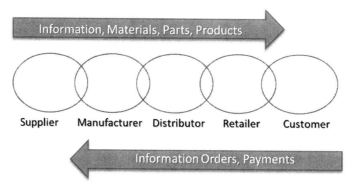

FIGURE 1-1 · Basic linear supply chain model.

supply chain management focus aligns objectives and performance metrics, and thus integrates these functions and fosters collaboration toward a common goal.

A Chain of Supply

In whatever way it is defined, the purpose of a chain of supply is to transform and transport whatever is required to meet customers' needs. It can be illustrated as a chain along which materials, products, information, and financial resources are moved in a system that creates and delivers a product or service; however, movement along the chain is not all downstream.

At the same time, a reverse flow travels from customers back up the supply chain. For example, information about customer preferences and firm orders drive the planning activities; payments by the customer fuel the whole process by covering costs and generating profits for the upstream providers. A basic linear supply chain diagram in Figure 1-1 represents just the major members included in a larger system.

Supply Chain Networks

The definition of supply chain management as used in this book provides a great deal of latitude. That's because there is no one type of supply chain. Supply chains and the management of them vary by industry, markets served, and products and services provided.

In addition to having multiple upstream suppliers, each member of the chain also has many customers. This creates a network of interdependent organizations and processes in a larger system. The term *supply chain network* is often

Get up – get dressed – get coffee – drive to work – arrive at office

FIGURE 1-2 · Getting-to-work linear model.

used instead of *supply chain* because a network better illustrates the realities of what actually exists.

Every firm in the chain has many interdependent relationships with suppliers and subcontractors who also have their own numerous suppliers and customers. Each of these groups creates different networks of both internal and external relationships. The important point of this model is to view any supply chain as a system—not as a group of individual entities doing its own thing.

The difference between a simple supply chain and a supply chain network can be illustrated by looking at something familiar—the process of getting to work or school. Figure 1-2 is a simplified diagram showing that linear process.

But, does it represent what really happens? The reality of what usually happens in just the early stages of the process—getting up and on the road—probably resembles the list of activities in Table 1-1.

As shown in the table, what happens is much more detailed and complex than the simple "Getting-to-work" diagram in Figure 1-2 suggests. A map of what actually takes place probably looks more like spaghetti, as in Figure 1-3, than like a nice neat chain.

TABLE 1-1 Starting the Process of Getting to Work or School		
1. Alarm sounds	2. Wake up	3. Hit alarm—snooze
4. Get up late	5. Run downstairs	6. Turn on coffee maker
7. Return to bedroom	8. Go to shower	9. Shower
10. Return to bedroom	11. Get dressed	12. Go back to kitchen
13. Start to get coffee	14. Go back to bedroom	15. Get forgotten tie
16. Return to kitchen	17. Pour coffee in mug	18. Leave house
19. Enter garage	20. Go back to house	21. Get cell phone
22. Leave house	23. Enter garage	24. Open garage door
25. Back car from garage	26. Close garage door	27. Reopen garage door
28. Get trash cans	29. Move cans to street	30. Return to car
31. Back car from driveway		

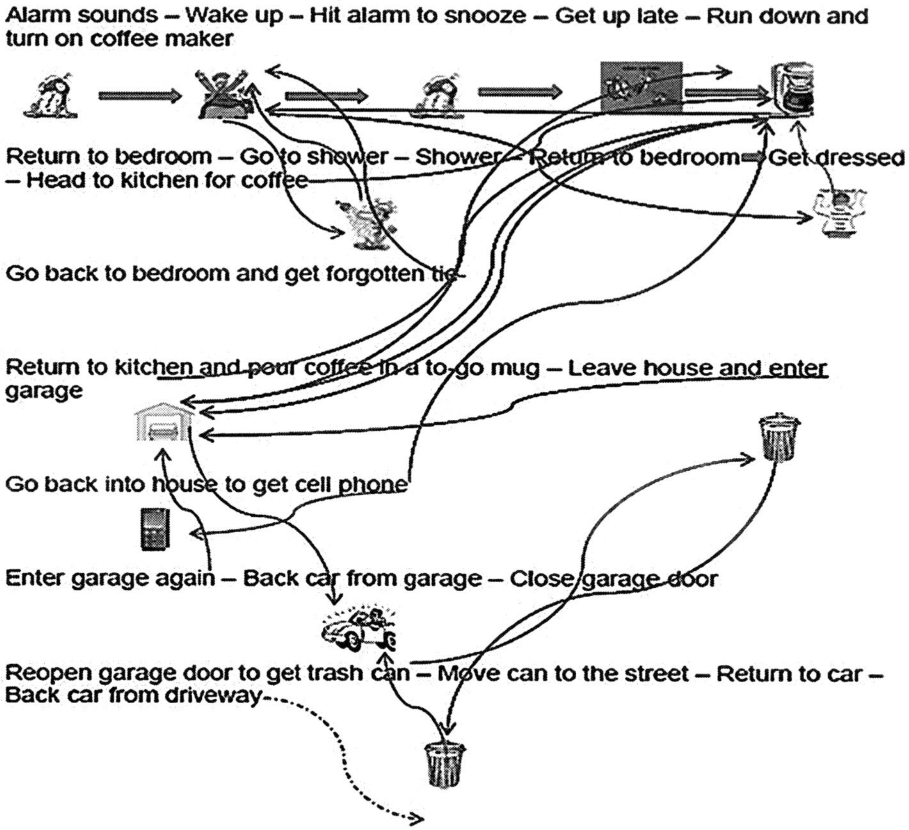

Alarm sounds – Wake up – Hit alarm to snooze – Get up late – Run down and turn on coffee maker

Return to bedroom – Go to shower – Shower – Return to bedroom – Get dressed – Head to kitchen for coffee

Go back to bedroom and get forgotten tie

Return to kitchen and pour coffee in a to-go mug – Leave house and enter garage

Go back into house to get cell phone

Enter garage again – Back car from garage – Close garage door

Reopen garage door to get trash can – Move can to the street – Return to car – Back car from driveway

FIGURE 1-3 · The getting-to-work real process.

Assume that supply chains are not so inefficient that their diagrams look like spaghetti or that their interconnected processes look like the reality of getting to work. However, as illustrated in Figure 1-4, supply chains are often much more complex than a linear diagram implies. The next chapter will explore the various members of this network and what they do.

Demand Chains and Value Chains

The concepts of *demand chain* and *value chain* shift the focus from upstream suppliers to the customer. The "demand" in a demand chain is from customers who want goods and services. As information about customer orders or anticipated requirements flows up the supply chain, members of the chain respond by providing those goods and services the customers are known to want. Rather than pushing products into the market, goods and services are pulled through by customer demand, as shown in Figure 1-5.

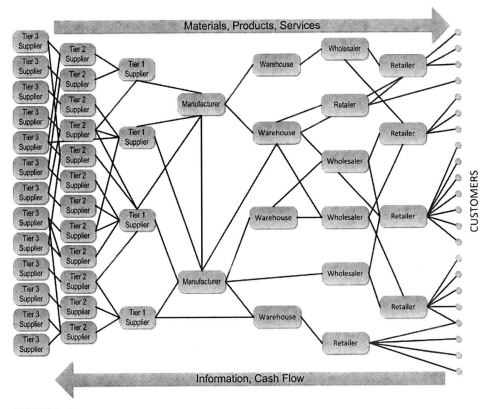

FIGURE 1-4 • A complex supply chain network.

In Michael Porter's insightful 1985 book *Competitive Advantage*, he demonstrated that firms could differentiate themselves through value-adding activities that benefit the customer. The more efficient and effective the firm is in performing such activities, the more opportunities there are to provide value for the customer.

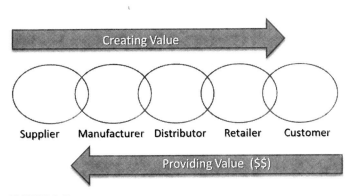

FIGURE 1-5 • Value chain model.

To manage a value chain requires an understanding of what's considered valuable. The final customer's perceptions about the value of anything are subjective. So firms must first determine what it is about a product or service that customers see as valuable and then the relative level of value placed on those attributes. The answers to three questions help to figure this out:

1. Who are the customers?
2. What is it they consider valuable?
3. What are the circumstances in which they make that determination?

Still Struggling

For example, gold is considered very valuable. In 2013, the prevailing price for a ten-gram nugget would be about $450.00. This is quite a lot for something smaller than a kernel of popcorn. Obviously, many people consider gold to have a relatively high value, which means that people would expect to receive something of a similarly high value for that nugget if they used it in a transaction.

Suppose your car broke down on the way to work. Someone stops to offer you a ride in exchange for some "gas money," but all you have in your pocket is that little gold nugget. Would you exchange it for a ride? Of course not. Your options are many and the relative value of the exchange would be vastly distorted. You could wait for a police officer to stop, call a tow truck if you have a cell phone, hitchhike and hope for a more compassionate driver, or maybe just walk. In any case, because of the situation and the available options, you do not see the value of the service—a ride to work—worth the value you place on your gold.

However, if your car broke down on a desolate stretch of unpaved desert road and you'd had nothing to eat or drink for many hours, the situation might be different. You might then consider trading a ride for the $450 value of the gold. It would be worth the exchange. In both instances you are the customer, the monetary value of the gold is the same, and the type of service to be provided is the same. However, you as the customer make different determinations of relative value based upon the circumstances in which the exchange takes place. Porter defined value as whatever a customer was willing to pay for a company's product or service. One of the factors that contributes to a person's perception of value is the context in which the decision is made.

Such evaluations are similar to the judgments firms must make in developing their supply chain strategies. They must know the context in which a customer is going to assess the value of their product or service and must consider that knowledge in managing their supply chain activities. This is not easy. Customers are individuals, and they do not all want the exact same products or services. Firms must use some kind of method to group together customers who have similar requirements and value expectations.

Customer Segmentation

Customer segmentation is one way to determine customers' similarities and differences. By segmenting customers into groups, firms can then identify and develop targeted opportunities to differentiate the products or services they offer. They would accomplish this by using specific supply chain strategies for different segments, which is key to using the supply chain to create competitive advantage. Chapter 3 will look more closely at customer segmentation as an element in developing supply chain strategies.

What customers consider valuable is most important. However, in addition to their perceptions of value, there are at least three other viewpoints that should be considered:

1. Value of each activity in the supply chain
2. Value from the organization's perspective
3. Value to society at large (This will be discussed in Chapter 9, "Corporate Social Responsibility.")

Value-adding activities in the supply chain are those that

- help transform materials into a product as it moves through the chain,
- are something the customer wants and is willing to pay for, and
- enhance the customer's evaluation of the product's worth.

Non-value-adding activities are those that do not meet these criteria. That is, they do not directly contribute to the final product or service the customer wants. For instance, customers don't want to pay for the costs of excess inventories, poor transportation choices that inflate costs, redundant activities such as warehousing and storage in multiple locations or by multiple organizations, the expediting of materials, or shortfalls in production.

To the extent possible, all members of the supply chain benefit when non-value-adding activities are eliminated or minimized. The total revenue received from providing customers with products or services minus the costs of doing so creates profit. The more efficient and effective a firm and its supply chain are in fulfilling customer requirements, the more profitable they will be.

Brand versus Component Value

The Swatch Group owns a subsidiary known as *ETA SA Swiss Watch Manufacturer*, or *ETA*. Most Swiss-made watches, including many expensive brands, have movements made by ETA. These brand-name firms design and assemble their watches but do not manufacture the internal workings of their products. Because they use the same supplier, they really have no functional differentiation among their products. Therefore, the brands must compete through design characteristics and marketing efforts. In this case, better collaboration with a critical upstream supplier isn't going to improve the value of a firm's individual products.

The same is often true in the automotive supply chain. Manufacturers may use the same suppliers, and sometimes they even supply each other with parts, subassemblies, or components. When the supplier is a competitor or a company that provides similar parts or products to a competitor, the likelihood that collaboration between the buying and supplying firms can create exclusive value is diminished. For instance, knowledge shared with a supplier about proprietary processes, designs, or materials can be legally protected by nondisclosure agreements, but it cannot be erased from the minds of the people who know it.

Both Advanced Micro Devices (AMD) and Intel supply computer manufacturers with the microprocessors that are the heart of the machine. Both suppliers market the relative benefits of their products to equipment manufacturers and the general public. This type of marketing promotes sales to equipment manufacturers and builds awareness in the final customer's mind. The processors themselves do not always give any single computer manufacturer a differentiating advantage other than what might come from a possible customer brand preference.

To attain a competitive advantage, a supply chain network's structure and its processes must be segmented, aligned with the markets served, and managed collaboratively. Dependent on their market's characteristics, such as customer buying patterns, larger firms might have more than one supply chain or supply chain network to manage.

Service Supply Chains

The service sector dominates the U.S. economy. Service firms offer "intangible products," such as utilities, transportation, warehousing, information, finance, insurance, education, health care, and entertainment. Both firms and individuals provide services to customers. Some refer to their customers as patients or clients, but the objective is the same—customer satisfaction. Whether as an organization, such as a dental clinic, or as an individual, such as a dentist in private practice, each provider requires some type of external resources in order to deliver services.

These resources include office equipment, supplies, software, utilities, vehicles, and so on. There is an easily identifiable flow of inputs that helps sustain a service provider's capabilities. Some of these inputs are directly tied to a particular service; others provide the necessary overhead infrastructure. Whatever the purpose, there is clearly an upstream chain that moves supplies toward the service provider. This means supply chain management techniques can be applied to that chain of supply. In fact, supply chain management for industries such as healthcare is a major factor in controlling costs and improving service.

Firms in all industry sectors have supply chains, but with similarities and differences. Common supply chain models do not neatly apply to firms that provide a service because the nature of services is very different from that of goods or products. Services are *intangible*, which means they cannot be seen or touched. Although the results of a service may be tangible, what the customer actually pays for is labor—either intellectual or physical. Of course services cannot be held in inventory either. They are both provided and consumed at the same time. This attribute adds an entirely different dimension to the process of fitting a service firm into a supply chain management framework.

One of the most important differences between product and service supply chains is in the role of the customer. In the manufacturing sector, it is easy to see the flow of materials from suppliers through a manufacturer's facility and then out the door into distribution and on to the final customer. In a manufacturing model, the customer has had no direct role in creating the product.

But this is not so with services. When purchasing services, the customer is both a supplier to that individual or service firm and a recipient of the service provided. The customer must supply some of the inputs required for the service provider to engage in the activity for which the customer is paying. For instance, obtaining the service may require the customer to be physically present, as in getting a haircut or consulting with a psychologist. Some services require the customer to provide an item or a belonging. Obviously, to have clothes dry-cleaned, the customer must first deliver the clothing to the dry cleaner; to have a car repaired, it must be taken to a mechanic.

Academics refer to this as the *customer-supplier duality* in providing services. That means that the inputs required for the service to be delivered flow in both directions—from the customer to the provider and from the provider to the customer. Unfortunately, unlike inputs to a manufacturing chain, the quality of customer inputs is variable and difficult to control.

What does this mean to service firms? Supply chain management methods are directly applicable to acquiring the resources that service providers need. But at the point of delivering the service to the customer, it's more about managing a relationship than a chain of supply. Table 1-2 summarizes key input and output differences between manufacturing and service firms.

TABLE 1- 2 Manufacturing versus Services	
Inputs • Labor • Materials • Capital equipment	Both types of firms need these three inputs. The difference is that most manufacturing labor is needed to manage all the activities required to get the material inputs, transform them into products and move them to customers. The cost of the inputs can be 50% or more of the products created. Capital equipment costs are also high for large scale manufacturing operations. In service firms labor is the major cost component. Materials include only what is needed to provide the service and capital costs are often minor compared to manufacturing. (Of course this varies widely by type of services offered.)
Outputs • Physical product • Customer satisfaction	Essentially both types of firms want to delight their customers. The difference is that manufactures do it by creating something tangible. Service firms do it by completing the activity for which they were hired. Educators help transform knowledge, banks facilitate financial transactions, insurance agencies protect against the consequences of a loss.

Still Struggling

Consider a situation in which a patient with a toothache goes to a dentist. Both patient and dentist share information. The dentist asks questions, and the patient responds with answers:

> Dentist: "Which tooth hurts?"
> Patient: "My upper right molar."
> Dentist: "When did you first notice pain?"
> Patient: "Last Friday after dinner."
> Dentist: "May I take an x-ray?"
> Patient: "Sure."
> Dentist: "Are you allergic to Novocain?"
> Patient: "No."

After this exchange of information, the dentist will locate the offending tooth, diagnose the problem, and perform the necessary procedures to remedy the problem. So, the customer (patient) supplied the following:

- His or her body (mouth)
- Information (answers to the questions that were required for the service to be performed)

The customer also received the output of the service:

- A repaired tooth (the deliverable from the service)
- Elimination of the pain (provided value)

The dentist received information necessary to perform the service and supplied the following:

- Expertise in dentistry (intellectual labor)
- Performance of the procedure (physical labor)
- Equipment needed for the service
- The materials associated with filling a tooth

Also, the dentist was compensated for having performed the service (received value).

The patient and the dentist made exchanges that required them to collaborate in having the service completed, as Figure 1-6 shows.

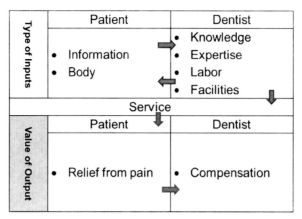

FIGURE 1-6 · Patient-dentist exchanges.

The Importance of Supply Chain Management

The present globalized business environment offers expanding market opportunities but also causes enormous competitive pressures and adds complexity to the supply chain. For example, competition forces ongoing efforts to reduce costs through low-cost country sourcing and the outsourcing of noncore activities. But sourcing from countries around the world with varied distribution patterns increases the length and complexity of the supply chains.

To overcome these challenges and meet today's ever-changing and more demanding customer expectations, the effective management of the supply chain network is critical. Somehow, all the members of the network must maximize communication and collaboration in order to meet their mutual objectives. These objectives have expanded from a list of "rights" that were first applied to the logistics function. They are now frequently referred to as the *Seven Rights of Supply Chain Management*:

1. The right product or service
2. To the right customer
3. In the right place
4. At the right time
5. In the right condition
6. At the right quantity
7. For the right cost

Three Major Forces

Three major forces affect a firm's ability to meet the essential objectives enumerated in the seven rights above:

1. Globalization
2. Technology
3. Customer expectations

Globalization

The global integration of economics, financials, trade, and communications has led to an increase in cross-border financial flows, the movement of entire industries to offshore locations, and an increase in the levels of international commerce. Producers of both goods and services in the United States now have to compete in local markets with firms from around the world. This trend has created additional pressure to reduce, or at least control, costs, which in turn, has forced some companies to abandon U.S.-based production altogether.

During the last few decades, many U.S. firms have moved operations offshore in a chase for the cheaper labor supplied by low-cost countries. But escalating labor rates in those countries continue to change the equation. The focus has become more about expanding in those foreign markets rather than just about seeking better pricing for parts and materials. A challenge for supply chain professionals is how to analyze the best offshore locations or, at least, how to be part of the decision-making process that does so.

The amount of global commercial activity, the speed with which it has grown, and the many risks involved also make globalization a key driver of supply chain planning and design. As suppliers and customers are created in faraway locations, the ability to manage effectively and efficiently the complexity of the resulting supply chain networks is a challenge. Meeting customers' ever-changing expectations for variety and their demands for immediate availability is complicated by the need to manage lead times, inventories, and product introductions across a global network of suppliers.

Technology

The applied use of science or knowledge toward commercial and industrial purposes is one way to define technology. Most often, the term is used as a general reference to the products, particularly electronic and digital, that are created through the application of science and knowledge. From a supply chain management perspective, both points of view are useful.

Supply chain management is both a driver of technological innovation and a means of integrating technological innovations into commerce. These are among the major technological innovations that have enabled much of the gains in supply chain efficiencies:

- *Internet-based communications* provide both synchronous and asynchronous access to information. *Synchronous* means that the communication taking place between those involved is in real time and includes contacts made through chat forums, video conferencing, and voice over IPs (VoIPs). *Asynchronous* communication allows people to connect at their convenience. Websites and email are asynchronous. Communication is a key to supply chain collaboration. Without this technology, our modern commerce would grind to a halt.

- *Global positioning systems (GPS)* include a network of satellites that broadcast signals read by devices on the ground. The system can usually pinpoint the location of a person or an object anywhere on earth. This has had a major impact in making transportation networks more efficient.

- *Radio frequency identification (RFID)* is a system for identifying and tracking materials. The technology is based on a small tag that has stored data and read/write capabilities. The tag also has an antenna to communicate that data to a reading device. The increasing use of RFID has greatly improved the process of tracking and communicating information about materials throughout the supply chain. The system promises to be one of the most important additions to supply chain infrastructure ever implemented.

- *Electronic funds transfer (ETF)* is a system used to transfer money between bank accounts. The system has eliminated much of the non-value-adding paperwork and processing costs incurred in the payment of invoices.

- *e-Commerce* can be simply defined as the buying and selling of goods and services on the Internet. It includes business-to-business (B2B) and business-to-consumer (B2C) transactions. An all-encompassing term, e-commerce is often used to incorporate the many aspects of B2B activities that now exist. From the sourcing of materials to the marketing to customers, e-commerce has had a tremendous impact on global businesses and their supply chain networks.

- *Enterprise resource planning (ERP) software* is a business management software program. Using a system of integrated applications, this software allows the sharing of information from a central database. The use of ERP systems has helped to improve the access to and availability of information across all internal functions. Manufacturing, planning, sales, purchasing, accounting, and marketing can all be integrated if the necessary applications (modules) have been purchased from the software's supplier. The system also provides an efficient way to manage contacts and information flow with the external supply chain members.

A growing multitude of hand-held devices will also continue to enhance and improve supply chain communication resources. By vastly improving interactions, planning capabilities, and the visibility of consumer buying patterns, these technologies have already fostered the rapid evolution of supply chain management over the last couple of decades. As a result, non-value-adding elements, such as long lead times and excessive inventories, have often been reduced or eliminated. This has decreased the costs and increased the efficiency of the system required to meet customer demands.

Although ongoing technological innovations will continue to benefit supply chain management strategies and practices, there are some downsides. The coordination and integration of all this technology does create more complexity in the supply chain network.

Customer Expectations

"I want it all, I want it all, I want it all—and I want it now!" Nothing better exemplifies today's customer expectations than that line by the legendary Freddie Mercury of the rock band "Queen." His lyrics were not far from what organizations face in trying to satisfy customers. A short, five item list of their expectations includes:

1. High quality products and services
2. Competitive prices
3. Immediate availability
4. Great service
5. Lots of choices

To further complicate the task faced by producers, no two customers are alike. Expectations regarding a host of attributes, such as quality, reliability, performance, longevity, and so on, vary from person to person. While we can't assess the impact of every possible customer expectation on supply chain management, a brief review of the five expectations listed above will illustrate some of the challenges they present.

1. Creating high quality products and services requires:
   - An in-depth knowledge of what the customer defines as "quality"
   - An integrative process of product development that brings together all the necessary internal and external players
   - Product or service design that maximizes value without adding cost
   - Efficient and effective production or service delivery operations

2. Offering competitive prices requires:
   - Knowledge of the market and the competitors in it
   - An understanding of cost drivers and how to aggressively manage them
   - Close collaboration with all key suppliers
   - Elimination of waste (non-value-adding elements)

3. Assuring immediate availability requires:
   - Accurate planning and forecasting
   - Balancing available capacity, utilization rates, and demand
   - Managing inventory throughout the supply chain
   - Utilizing the right channels of distribution

4. Delivering great service requires:
   - Understanding the customer's perception of the service
   - Knowing which attributes are most important to the customer
   - Staffing appropriately to meet customer expectations
   - Training staff
   - Selecting the right outsourced service providers

5. Providing lots of choices requires:
   - Innovative and continuous research and development
   - An increase in the number of stock-keeping units (SKUs)
   - A proliferation in the number of separate items for which planning and forecasting are required
   - A way to overcome competition for shelf space in the retail sector

Of course this is but a small list of customer expectations and the ways in which firms must respond to accommodate them. The important point is just to demonstrate that the most effective ways to assure customer satisfaction all require an integrative approach—a supply chain management perspective.

That idea may have started out as just a way to help reduce costs, but it is now considered a critical factor in the success of any business.

Summary

Supply chain management is a concept that is still being developed. It's more of a philosophy than a rigid set of rules. That philosophy deals with integrating all the players and what they do into an efficient means of providing customers with the right products and services. Many definitions and models exist for supply chains and supply chain management. What they all have in common is the need to break down internal and external barriers that impede communication and collaboration toward common goals.

The supply chain management concept can be applied to both products and services. Service providers have an upstream chain of supply that can be managed. However, customers play a direct role in the actual delivery of the services they buy. This dynamic creates a relationship between the service provider and the customer that is more than the usual addition of links to the chain.

The idea that supply chains must add value for their customers has moved the focus from the supply side of the model to the customer side. Firms need to understand what their customers think is valuable and work to eliminate anything in the supply chain that does not contribute to it. By segmenting customer groups according to their preferences, firms can design their supply chain strategies to meet specific sets of customer expectations. This can create valuable competitive advantages in the marketplace.

QUIZ

1. Supply chain management is_____
   A. a set of rules.
   B. more of a philosophy.
   C. a software system.
   D. a board game.

2. Supply chain management has _____
   A. a customer focus.
   B. no value
   C. little collaboration.
   D. no purpose.

3. Supply chain management stresses _____
   A. collaboration.
   B. confrontation.
   C. production.
   D. low prices.

4. Many supply chain definitions focus on ____
   A. lower prices from suppliers.
   B. manufacturing.
   C. global business.
   D. government rules.

5. Which statement is true?
   A. Services supply chains are different from manufacturing ones.
   B. Supply chain management cannot be used in service firms.
   C. Services do not require inputs from customers.
   D. Dentists do not provide services.

6. Which statement explains the meaning of *supply chain collaboration?*
   A. Many individual firms work together.
   B. Firms must work with governments.
   C. Only retail firms collaborate.
   D. Supply chain members team up for parties.

7. Which statement is true?
   A. All supply chain models are the same.
   B. There is no difference between service and product supply chains.
   C. Supply chain members must join an association.
   D. Supply chains vary by industry.

8. **Which statement explains the meaning of *supply chain network*?**
   A. Chains are only as strong as their weakest link.
   B. A network model is linear.
   C. There are many processes and many interconnected members.
   D. It is more like a television network.

9. **A benefit from a supply chain management system can be _____**
   A. a competitive advantage.
   B. increased costs.
   C. more inventory.
   D. no customer service.

10. **Value is added when _____**
    A. a process is inefficient.
    B. supply chain members compete.
    C. customers decide what is valuable.
    D. labor is done offshore.

11. **A customer's perception of "value" is _____**
    A. pretty much the same for everyone.
    B. based on the context or situation.
    C. not something that can be measured.
    D. not an important factor.

12. **The objectives of the "Seven Rights" include the _____**
    A. right forecast.
    B. right place.
    C. right people.
    D. right supplies.

13. **The segmentation of customers is important because _____**
    A. people like to be grouped together.
    B. it can influence supply chain strategy and design.
    C. it is an easier process than looking for offshore market opportunities.
    D. it is the law.

14. **Globalization has _____**
    A. changed supply chain management.
    B. not been an approved practice.
    C. offered nothing new.
    D. stopped.

15. **Supply chain management is important because _____**
    A. global competition is easy.
    B. supply chains have become longer.
    C. customers are all the same.
    D. it is in the news.

chapter **2**

Supply Chain Collaboration

Supply chain collaboration is a hot topic of business conversations. However, talking about collaboration is easier than doing it. Supply chain collaboration depends on people working together—both inside and outside an organization. There are always challenges in getting a group of people to be a team and not just a collection of individuals.

CHAPTER OBJECTIVES

In this chapter, you will learn

- What collaboration is.
- Who the major internal and external members of the chain of supply are.
- What role they each play in the supply chain.
- What responsibilities and activities are associated with both internal and external supply chain members.
- Why internal and external collaboration is important.
- What types of collaborative methods are used.
- How organizations can do it.

One example of successful collaboration is usually found in a sports team. Putting a group of people onto the field and telling them to "play ball" would not be very effective. Getting the players to work together requires everyone to know what the game plan is, to know their role in that plan, and to cooperate as they perform the actions their roles require. Each team member must also have the knowledge, skills, equipment, and incentives necessary to work as a team and head toward the same goal. It's really no different in a supply chain—the same requirements and the same problems arise in making supply chain collaboration happen. Just like in a ball game, getting different people and organizations on the team and in alignment is a challenge. The effort can be costly, and the results are not always certain.

We will begin by defining supply chain collaboration, explaining why it is important, and then exploring the issues that help or hinder collaboration efforts. In order to do that, we'll also identify the principal members of a supply chain, review their roles and responsibilities, and propose some ideas about how to make collaboration happen.

What Is Collaboration?

The phrase *supply chain collaboration* represents the collective interactions of supply chain members toward achieving a mutually beneficial goal. *Collective interactions* refers to the ways in which the members communicate, share information, engage in joint planning and decision making, and coordinate their activities. The term *mutually beneficial* means that each member stands to gain something from working together.

The Importance of Collaboration

Supply chain collaboration is important because efficiency and effectiveness in supply chain operations are especially critical in today's dynamic global economy. Ways to reduce costs and create competitive advantage are vital for success. Collaboration among supply chain members is seen as one approach that contributes to both objectives.

Collaboration can surely help drive out cost and waste in the supply chain, but it is more than that alone. When parties work together, the relationships become less about price and more about value. Value can be shared and passed through to customers for competitive advantage. Close working relationships also improve risk management, as we'll see in Chapter 7.

As illustrated in Figure 2-1, the goal will be the same, but the reasons why each member works toward it need not be.

- A common goal is one that is identical for all members. Meeting customers' demands in order to make a profit is an example of a common goal.

- A shared goal is one, such as cost savings, in which more than one member benefits but those benefits may not be equally distributed.

- Joint goals are those in which the members seek the same results but for different reasons. A manufacturer might want to increase market share for a product through more competitive pricing. To reduce product costs, the company outsources production to a supplier whose goal is to increase business.

In each case, the end result toward which everyone is working is identical. Reaching a goal that advances the interests of each party is the purpose of working together.

The extent to which supply chain members collaborate ranges from modest activities to very complex integrated projects. In the external supply chain, *vendor managed inventories* (VMI) is a method that has been around for many years and is usually a small-scale operation. Essentially, VMI requires the sharing of information about the requirements, inventory levels, and anticipated demand between the buying firm and one or just a few suppliers. However, methods, such as *efficient consumer response* (ECR), used by consumer goods companies and grocery retailers are much larger in scale and complexity. The number of items to be collaboratively managed can be extensive. It requires the capture of point-of-sale data at the retail level and the circulation of that data throughout the upstream supply chain. This information then becomes a com-

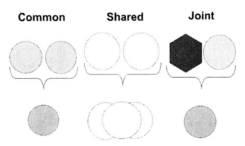

FIGURE 2-1 · Types of goals.

ponent in the entire supply chain's decision-making processes about manufacturing and distribution.

Internally, personnel from many functional areas related to supply chain activities cooperate in strategic, tactical, and operational decisions that include planning, forecasting, and scheduling. This interaction can range from high-level supply chain strategy development to *sales and operations planning* (S&OP) or to daily status meetings. The possibilities for internal collaboration will be demonstrated later in this chapter.

Supply Chain Members

When discussing supply chain collaboration, the first question is, "Who are members of a supply chain and what do they do?" The answer, of course, is "it depends." Which supply chain is being discussed? Supply chain strategies are often designed to meet specific customer groups, and each strategy could require a different supply chain with its own membership needs, as seen in Chapter 3. Additionally, a supply chain has both internal and external members with individual functional roles and responsibilities. For simplicity, the examples provided here reflect a typical manufacturing supply chain.

Internal Supply Chain Membership

The size of an organization and the industry sector in which it operates are major factors in determining who the internal players are. Small manufacturing operations may have one person who wears many hats and has functional responsibilities for several supply chain areas. In larger firms, the duties in these areas would each be performed by separate groups that include: marketing, supply management, finance, production, logistics, and *information technology* (IT). Other internal players, such as the legal, human resources, and customer service departments, are important, but the activities of the first six are key factors in managing the supply chain.

Marketing

In his book *The Practice of Management*, legendary management guru Peter Drucker wrote: "Because the purpose of business is to create and keep a customer, the business enterprise has two, and only two, basic functions: marketing and innovation. Marketing and innovation produce results; all the rest are costs. Marketing is the distinguishing, unique function of the business." According to Drucker, marketing's basic function is "...to attract and retain customers at a profit." Said another way, marketing must profitably identify, forecast, and satisfy customers' needs and wants.

To accomplish that goal, marketing personnel manage four elements in a marketing mix: *product*, *price*, *place*, and *promotion*. These "4Ps" have been expanded over the years and now often include others, such as *people*, *process*, and *physical evidence* (packaging and placement).

1. *Product*—Whatever satisfies the needs or wants of a customer is a product. This may be a tangible good or an intangible service.

2. *Price*—Expressed as an amount of money, this is whatever the buyer and seller agree upon to make the exchange for a product.

3. *Place*—This is primarily concerned with distribution. Successful marketing requires getting the right product to the right place for customers.

4. *Promotion*—This is communication; marketing must inform and persuade. The many ways in which marketing gets the message out about its products and attempts to encourage a customer's desire for them include: public relations, press releases, advertising, direct marketing, and personal selling (word of mouth).

5. *People*—This refers to all the people involved in the exchange of products and services and includes the customers and the internal employees whose customer service and relationship-developing skills help build customer loyalty and differentiate a firm.

6. *Process*—All the tasks, procedures, and polices that assist in getting a product or service to the customer are part of the process. Process also includes the methods in place for providing customer service. Communicating and interacting with customers, receiving orders, and handling complaints are just a few of the many customer related processes in marketing.

7. *Physical evidence (packaging and placement)*—Packaging not only encloses and protects a product as it travels through the chain of supply; it also influences the customer's buying decisions. Therefore, the size, shape, color, graphics, and many more visual attributes of packaging need to be addressed. In retail operations, the "physical" aspects also apply to the layout of the store and the positioning of displays.

Example: Supply Chain Collaboration in Packaging and Placement

There are different levels and types of packaging that require attention from a supply chain perspective. At a basic level, packaging is whatever is used to enclose and protect a product until it gets to the final consumer. It can add unacceptable cost and little customer value if not properly designed.

Retail-ready packaging is a rather recent European import to the United States. Retail-ready packaging serves the protection purposes of conventional packaging but allows a retailer to use it as part of a shelf display. For instance, candy bars located at the grocery checkout counter are displayed in retail-ready packaging. The individual candy bars arrive in boxes that may be opened and immediately displayed.

Sounds great, right? Well, yes, but many factors need to be coordinated among supply chain members from the producer to the final customer before this becomes a "great" idea.

- From the producer, shipper, and warehousing perspectives, issues such as the quality, size, and weight of the packages to be shipped are important.
- From the retailer's perspective, the ease of use, shelf-space requirements, simplicity of product identification, and the quantity of waste to be disposed of or recycled are important concerns.
- Customers just want it easy.... They want to see it, be able to grab it, and be able to put it back on the shelf without any hassle.

It is a good idea, but there's no way of meeting everyone's needs without a high degree of collaboration up and down the supply chain.

Supply Management

The primary function of supply management is to identify and obtain all the external resources necessary to support the activities of the firm. This is equally true for both manufacturing and service firms. In either case, supply management must ensure that everything necessary for the firm to produce products or provide services and support operations is available when and where required.

There are four terms that organizations frequently use to identify the business department responsible for buying materials and services. They are:

purchasing, procurement, sourcing, and supply management. In this book, we use the term "supply management," which the *Institute for Supply Management* (ISM) defines as, "The identification, acquisition, access, positioning, management of resources and related capabilities the organization needs or potentially needs in the attainment of its strategic objectives." It is the most inclusive term and, therefore, the most appropriate definition of what the function does today.

Supply management has both strategic and tactical responsibilities. Strategic duties are those that involve greater long-term and financial consequences for a firm. One of these is *supplier relationship management* (SRM). SRM is a vital activity and among supply management's most important duties in supply chain management. This topic will be explored further in Chapter 4. Tactical duties are those that deal with the daily operational aspects of acquiring the goods and services that keep the wheels turning in a company. Examples of these two sets of activities are outlined in Table 2-1.

Supply management's essential strategic role in managing a supply chain network will be fully examined in Chapter 4.

Organizational Structure

The way in which the supply management function is organized varies widely, depending upon the size and nature of the firm. It would be best if a firm's supply management staff and its organizational structure reflected best-in-class practices. In reality, the staff levels and organizational structure are usually made to fit the funds available for them.

TABLE 2-1 Supply Management's Strategic and Tactical Responsibilities

Strategic	Tactical
• Strategic planning	• Processing requisitions
• Category management	• Releasing orders
• Supplier sourcing	• Expediting parts and materials
• Make vs. buy and outsourcing decisions	• Processing receipts and invoices
• Contract negotiations and management	• Maintaining order records
• Cost analysis	• Processing *purchase orders* (P.O.s)
• *Supplier relationship management* (SRM)	
• Supplier quality assurance	

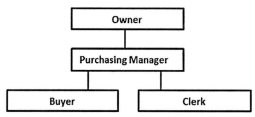

FIGURE 2-2 · Small business purchasing organization.

As illustrated in Figure 2-2, in smaller companies, someone may wear multiple hats with the title of purchasing manager among them. If there is an employee designated as a purchasing manager, that individual often reports directly to the owner and may have limited staff. In mid-size and larger firms, the supply management function will be a separate department with a senior or mid-level manager and various buying and support personnel. In larger firms, it is also common to see this group reporting to the head of supply chain management.

The separation of strategic and tactical duties is a key aspect of a supply management department's structure that should be established and maintained. While it may be possible for smaller firms to combine these responsibilities for one position, it's not advisable for larger firms to do so. When these duties are combined, it inevitably leads to suboptimal outcomes.

Finance

The finance department is the group that manages the firm's money. These are the people who write the checks. Finance has three critical functions: (1) to provide support for business and operational planning, (2) to provide operational support to the company's other functions, and (3) to produce required internal and external reports. Finance usually incorporates both financial management and accounting services.

Financial management includes the following activities:

- *Planning*—Financial strategies, budgeting, revenue and expense projections, and estimating the cost of capital projects.

- *Compliance*—Monitoring expenditure activity; assuring compliance with federal, state, and local regulations; assessing tax abatement methods and internal auditing to guarantee that company policies are met; and safeguarding against fraudulent activity.

- *Guidance*—Finance must provide management with quantitative data and well-supported recommendations to help them make decisions about projects, capital purchases, and investments.

- *Risk management*—Financial risks are serious concerns for an organization. To prevent damage to the firm, finance professionals work to identify and manage any risks. This may include managing risk through the use of insurance or other financial measures. (Supply chain risk management is discussed in Chapter 7.)

Accounting services include the following activities:

- *Tracking expenditures and revenue*—The accounting group is responsible for measuring and recording all business transactions. Every dollar that is spent or received must be tracked. Accounting is responsible to see that expense and revenue records are current and accurate. They are also responsible for billing customers.

- *Making payments*—Invoices from vendors and suppliers must be paid. Timely payment is often a requirement in order to get a discount from suppliers.

- *Creating reports for external use*—Includes reporting to the *Internal Revenue Service* (IRS), the *Securities and Exchange Commission* (SEC), and to shareholders. These reporting documents include balance sheets, profit and loss statements, and cash flow statements that are created according to *generally accepted accounting principles* (GAAP).

Production (Operations in Service Firms)

ISM defines operations as: "…the planning, scheduling and control of activities that transform inputs into products or services." However, the term production most often refers to what is done by manufacturers and producers. In service companies, such as banking, insurance, and healthcare, operations refers to the activities required to support the firm itself and the services it provides. Chapter 5 is devoted to more thoroughly illustrating production for each type of organization.

Logistics

The basic function of logistics is to manage the means by which an organization moves and stores products and materials from the extraction of raw commodities through the chain of supply to customers. Currently, the term logistics is associated more with a set of functions and activities that happen inside a company rather than with the larger or complete process. Supply chain management has become the accepted term for describing the management of all the activities, including logistics, which are required to bring something from earth to customer.

Firms may have a department responsible for all their logistics activities or they may have individual departments responsible for the various logistics functions. The core functions most often considered part of logistics will be addressed in Chapter 6.

Information Technology

Generally referred to as IT, this term is applied to both infrastructure and a department within a firm. The *infrastructure* refers to the electronic equipment (mainly computers), the systems used to store, retrieve, and analyze data, and the communications equipment used to transmit it. The internal supply chain members are the personnel responsible for managing that infrastructure. The IT group's basic function is to manage the means by which an organization collects, stores, processes, and communicates information.

The *IT department* serves many purposes. These professionals are in charge of assessing and making recommendations about equipment, working with service suppliers, determining system capacity requirements, and maintaining all the electronic communication and data processing assets of the firm. This includes both the hardware and the software required to run a business's applications, such as the ERP system, communication services, and desktop programs.

External Supply Chain Members

Manufacturer

A manufacturer is an individual or organization that transforms inputs to create a product. Individuals may do this by hand and organizations do it with machinery and personnel. The term can be applied to a company, a person, or a group of people.

Manufacturers are all producers, but not all producers are manufacturers. While it can represent a manufacturing firm, the word *producer* best describes the types of firms that *produce* the inputs to a manufacturing process. These could be raw materials, such as steel or milk or grains or some other intermediate good that becomes part of a final product. For example, steel is used to create

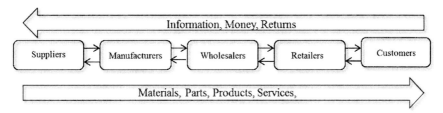

FIGURE 2-3 • Supply chain members are all suppliers in some way.

automobile body parts and milk is used to make cheese. Producers include builders, farmers, mining firms, consultants, brewers, and so on. Chapter 5 will more fully explain manufacturers and producers.

Suppliers

Suppliers are the external organizations or individuals that provide the goods, materials, and services that firms need to create their own products or services. As Figure 2-3 shows, every member of the supply chain is in some way a supplier.

The supply chain from the manufacturer back upstream is referred to as a "tier of suppliers." In this chain, the manufacturer is also known as the *original equipment manufacturer* or OEM. The OEM makes the final products that customers buy. Above the OEM in the chain are a series of supplier tiers, as shown in Figure 2-4.

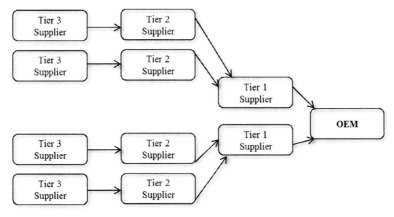

FIGURE 2-4 • Supplier tiers.

1. *Tier 1 suppliers* provide parts and materials directly to the OEM. For instance, Johnson Controls is a very large diversified firm with many divisions making both final goods and intermediate parts. Its battery division is a major supplier to the automotive industry. Johnson Controls' battery division is a first-tier supplier.

2. *Tier 2 suppliers* do not usually provide parts or materials directly to the OEM. Their role is primarily as a supplier to the tier 1 companies. A company that supplied Johnson Controls with packaging materials would be a tier 2 supplier.

Most often, the further the supplier is up the tier, the more likely it is that the supplier provides a basic raw material rather than a finished part or subassembly. An OEM will have many suppliers who also have suppliers and those suppliers have suppliers—comprising a supply network. As described in Chapter 1, this network can be very complex and interdependent.

Transporters (Transportation Service Providers)

The basic function of transporters is to move materials and goods from wherever they are to where they are needed, when they are needed. As noted previously in this section, transportation will be a major component of Chapter 6.

Wholesalers and Distributors

These two labels are frequently used interchangeably or sometimes even combined, such as in the reference to a *wholesale distributor*. A *wholesaler* serves as an intermediary between the manufacturer and the retailer, but how that intermediary's function is defined varies. One difference between wholesalers and distributors is that *distributors* may have direct business relationships with the manufacturer whose products they stock. This sometimes includes the exclusive right to offer a manufacturer's products in certain geographic regions. Wholesalers and retailers must then deal with the distributor for that manufacturer's products in order to purchase them for resale to other customers.

Wholesalers (or wholesale distributors) are categorized by the type of products they sell:

1. *Durable goods*—These are things that don't wear out quickly. They are items expected to last longer than three years. Durable goods can be of two types: consumer or commercial. Consumer durables are things such as cars, jewelry, office furniture, and washing machines. Commercial durables are things such as trucks, aircraft, and other heavy equipment.

2. *Nondurable goods*—These are products that usually don't last long, such as clothing, or things used quickly, such as cosmetics.

3. *Foodstuffs*—Anything with food value is considered *foodstuff*. The range of items in this category is enormous, but the word explains itself—everything from carrots to coconuts, lettuce to lemons, and doughnuts to dark chocolate.

However categorized, the primary purpose of both wholesalers and distributors is to buy in bulk and create smaller lots to be sold to their customers. In general, they purchase large quantities of products from manufacturers. These large lots are then sorted, repackaged, and distributed to customers in smaller lots. These customers are not ordinarily the final consumers. Instead, a wholesaler's customers are institutional, industrial, and retail operations. For example, a wholesaler's customer could be

- an institutional buyer employed by a public organization such as a school,

- a commercial buyer employed by a firm, or

- someone employed in merchandising or category management for a retailer.

Each of these customers purchases goods and materials from wholesalers on behalf of the organization for whom they work.

Usually, it's the retailers that sell items individually—for example, consumer goods or foodstuffs, such as a carton of milk, a six-pack of beverages, a toaster, etc. But wholesalers may also sell single items to industrial buyers. These sales are generally durable goods, such as large industrial equipment, tractors, cranes, forklifts, etc.

Depending upon the industry, wholesalers may not even be in the chain of supply. Apparel and other textile products are often sent directly to the retailer and don't pass through a wholesaler's warehouse. For example, Gap, Inc. is a major player in the garment industry. The company designs and markets clothing that is sold in thousands of Gap retail stores around the world. The manufacturing of these garments is done in countries such as Bangladesh, the Philippines, and Pakistan.

Gap has International Sourcing operations that oversee the production of its clothing at numerous facilities worldwide. A few key suppliers who have a multitiered network of material suppliers and subcontractors make the Gap's clothing. Once completed, the garments produced are shipped through one of

FIGURE 2-5 · A book supply chain.

Gap's International Sourcing offices, or more likely, directly to a Gap regional distribution center.

Still Struggling

If you're totally confused, there are flow charts in Figure 2-5, Figure 2-6, and Figure 2-7 that may help to illustrate the distributor-wholesaler's place in a supply chain. A book supply chain includes both a distributor and wholesalers. The distributor works with the publisher (manufacturer) and performs activities, such as warehousing and fulfillment of wholesale orders. The wholesalers sell to retail operations. An office furniture manufacturer may have an agreement with a wholesale distributor in a certain territory. Office furniture retailers buy from them. The Gap supply chain is an example of a direct from manufacturer to retailer flow..

Retailers

Any individual or business that sells goods or materials directly to consumers is a retailer. Table 2-2 lists just the major types of retail supply chain members. These can be categorized by the variety of products offered, level of service provided, and price as shown.

Customers

Merriam-Webster's Dictionary online provides interesting definitions for the word customer: "1. one that purchases a commodity or service; 2. an individual usually having some specified distinctive trait." These are both quite different from the

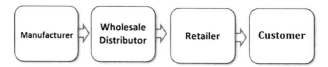

FIGURE 2-6 · Office furniture supply chain.

FIGURE 2-7 · Apparel supply chain.

dictionary's definition of a *consumer*, which is "one that utilizes economic goods." What the definitions offer is a very easy way to look at the distinctions between which supply chain members are customers and which are consumers.

When defined as one who purchases a commodity or service, the term *customer* includes everyone in the chain of supply. Is there really any difference between *customers* and *consumers*?

- Customers are the ones who pay for something—but they may not be the ones who actually consume or use it.
- Consumers are the ones who actually use the product or are the recipients of the benefit of a service.

In that sense, some supply chain members are both customers and consumers, e.g. suppliers, manufacturers, or producers. Wholesalers and distributors are customers but not consumers because they do not actually use the products they buy. Why is this of any importance? It is useful information because the needs

TABLE 2-2 Characteristics of Major Retail Types			
Retailers	**Price**	**Variety**	**Service Provided**
Warehouse (Big Box) Stores	Low	Wide	Low
Department Stores	Mid to High	Wide	Mid to High
Specialty Stores and Shops	Mid to High	Narrow	High
Convenience Stores	Mid to High	Narrow to Medium	Low
Supermarket Food Stores	Mid	Wide	Low
Outlet (Discount) Stores	Low	Narrow to Medium	Low
Restaurants	Low to High	Narrow	Low to High
Bars, Pubs	Low to High	Narrow	Low to High

of both customers and consumers must be satisfied throughout the supply chain. The reasons for keeping multiple perspectives about customers will become more evident in Chapter 3, "Supply Chain Strategies."

Supply Chain Collaboration

As noted in Chapter 1, supply chain management thinking brought a new perspective based on a vision of an extended enterprise, a complex system that included the internal and external supply chain members just reviewed. Meeting the need for supply chain member integration and collaboration has become a key aspect of supply chain management.

Internal Collaboration

What all of these internal supply chain members need to do is communicate and collaborate. They must collect, analyze, and communicate information and engage in joint decision-making processes. Unfortunately, many firms are still unable to overcome a silo approach to management inside their organizations. Departments tend to focus on their own narrow areas of responsibility and neglect the impact their actions and decisions may have on other internal departments. This means the departments will have difficulty collaborating with each other. If internal collaboration is not possible, external collaboration will be difficult.

The impediments to internal collaboration are often apparent. For instance, individual and departmental performance metrics within a firm may be set without regard to their impact across functions. In the supply management area, it's not uncommon that performance to standard cost is used as one of the metrics by which buying personnel are evaluated. A *standard cost* is an estimate of what a purchased item, part, material, or service is going to cost. It's used for budget purposes, developing prices, and valuating inventory.

The *purchase price* is what a company actually pays for something. The difference between what the estimated (standard) cost in the accounting system and the purchase price is called *purchase price variance* (PPV). If a buyer can purchase an item for less than the standard cost, that's a positive purchase price variance and considered a "good thing." But purchase price is only one element of total cost.

Suppose a buyer can get an item for $.90 that has a current standard cost of $1.00. Is that good? Didn't the buyer save 10 cents? Well maybe not. If that new supplier is somewhere offshore, the lead time may be long, the quantities required per order higher, the transportation and inventory carrying costs increased, and the supplier delivery time and quality uncertain. If the previous $1.00 purchases were made locally with a cooperative supplier, had no quality issues, and were delivered just as needed, the total cost for the $1.00 item may actually be much lower.

This is just one example of how performance measures can drive the wrong behavior. More details about overall supply chain metrics can be found in Chapter 9.

Still Struggling

Let's talk about beer. This is an example of how all the internal functions of a brewing operation need to collaborate in order to get you a new type of beer. Suppose a brewer's marketing department decides that there's a need for a new brew—maybe a low calorie, low carb, dark beer. Let's call it "Dusky Dark Ultra-lite" or "D2 Ultra" for short. Marketing's research shows that D2 Ultra needs to taste more like a microbrew or craft beer.

Customers already have many, many types and brands of beer from which to choose. So the marketing group believes that D2 Ultra can't be just another bland concoction invented by a committee trying to satisfy the most common beer drinker's taste buds and pocketbook. How's this going to happen? Who inside the brewing company needs to collaborate to create the recipe, produce the beer, and market and distribute it? Everybody does.

The majority of the cost and value of any product or service is established right up front in the design and development stage. Because of its importance, we'll cover this topic in detail later. For now, let's assume D2 Ultra has been developed and is ready to go into full-scale production.

At this point, two areas in which collaboration will be critically important are the sharing of information and joint decision making. Table 2-3 illustrates some of the issues that need to be covered.

What Everybody Needs to Know

Table 3-2 does not show everything that needs to happen. Here's a little more detail to demonstrate the importance of working together inside the brewing company.

TABLE 2-3 Requirements for Internal Collaboration, Functional Information Sharing, and Planning

Internal SC Member	Function	What Do They Need to Know?	Who Provides the Information?
Marketing	Attract and retain customers at a profit	• Supply constraints • Budget • Lead times • Production capacity	✓ Supply Management ✓ Finance ✓ Production ✓ Logistics
Supply Management	Ensure the supply of all the materials, parts, and services required	• Ingredients • Packaging • Time lines • Budget	✓ Marketing ✓ Finance ✓ Production ✓ Logistics
Finance	Manage the money	• Capital requirements • Revenue expectations • Product costs	✓ Marketing ✓ Supply Management ✓ Finance ✓ Production ✓ Logistics
Production	Produce and package beer	• Recipe • Process modifications • Volumes • Lead times • Product packaging	✓ Marketing ✓ Supply Management ✓ Logistics
Logistics	Manage the means by which the brewery moves and stores beer products	• Volumes • Distribution areas • Distribution channel • Lead times • Product packaging	✓ Marketing ✓ Supply Management ✓ Production
IT	Manage the means by which the brewery collects, stores, processes, and communicates information	• Impact to hardware and software requirements • Budget	✓ Marketing ✓ Supply Management ✓ Production ✓ Finance

What Marketing Needs to Know

1. *Supply constraints*—The supply management group needs to keep marketing abreast of changes in supply for ingredients such as hops and grain. Seasonality, weather, pricing, and lack of growers may impact availability.

2. *Budget*—The finance group needs to assess pricing and costs to determine the budget for the product.

3. *Lead times*—This is a function of both internal and external capabilities. Marketing needs to coordinate any product launch with supply management and production to assure that there is enough internal capacity and that there are external supplies and suppliers available.

4. *Production capacity*—Production needs to know the sales expectations and ensure there is capacity scheduled to meet them. Finance may be involved if there is a need for additional capital equipment to meet required capacity.

What Supply Management Needs to Know

1. *Ingredients*—What ingredients and in what quantity are two pieces of information needed to meet production requirements. Beer consists of just four basic ingredients: water, grain (usually barley), hops, and yeast. But there are many varieties of each of these ingredients. For instance, what type of malted barley will be used: pale, stout, amber, caramel, or some other? Production and marketing must work together to create a production plan that gives supply management information about types of materials, the quantity required, and when it's needed.

2. *Packaging*—What type of packaging and labeling will be needed? Once again, multiple internal functions have a hand in determining this: marketing, production, and logistics.

3. *Time lines*—Is there enough time to source the required ingredients and materials? In-store dates must be backed up to accommodate purchasing, production, and transportation lead times.

4. *Budget*—Marketing and sales determine price points for the products. However, the supply management group has to ensure that the purchase prices for ingredients and materials are consistent with the product cost targets. Production, marketing, finance, and logistics all need to collaborate in controlling those costs.

What Finance Needs to Know

1. *Capital requirements*—Is there enough capacity to produce D2 Ultra? Will additional equipment or warehouse space be needed? Marketing, production, logistics, and supply management all need to get involved in sharing this information and making recommendations about any action needed.

2. *Revenue expectations*—Marketing and sales set revenue expectations based upon price and volume. Finance needs to work with production, logistics, and supply management to ensure that the costs associated with each of their functions leaves an adequate margin for profit.

What Production Needs to Know

1. *Recipe*—The basic recipe for beer is pretty much the same. Variations in the brewing process and ingredients are primarily what make beers different. Supply management needs to tell production if there are any potential risks in getting those ingredients.

2. *Process modifications*—From marketing, the production group needs to know what product attributes they need to enhance.

3. *Volumes*—Capacity planning for equipment and personnel make accurate sales estimates important.

4. *Lead times*—When is it needed? Does production have the necessary time to produce the product and assure delivery when expected? Once again, marketing, sales, supply management, and logistics all need to work together to answer these questions.

5. *Product packaging*—Final product packaging, containers, and labels all need to be designed and created well ahead of production. The type of container and the filling and handling equipment available will also be an issue. Logistics will need to know what the industrial packaging configuration will be to incorporate that into their planning. Of course, supply management needs to get involved to see to it that this is all sourced and purchased in time.

What Logistics Needs to Know

1. *Volumes*—It's clear from all of the above that logistics needs to know how much of the beer and what packaging configurations should be expected. They get this from marketing, sales, and production.

2. *Distribution areas*—Is this to be a local, regional, national, or international launch? Logistics needs to know marketing's product roll-out strategy and timetable to be able to plan accordingly.

3. *Distribution channel*—Most beer in the United States needs to go through a three-tiered distribution system. It cannot be shipped directly to retail operations. These rules also vary by state and for international destinations. Once again, logistics needs to know how much, where it's going, and when.

4. *Lead times*—When is the product due in retail outlets? How much time will it sit in distribution before getting there? Logistics needs that information to plan the transportation mode and the carrier to be used.

5. *Product packaging*—Size and weight are big issues for logistics. Both impact transportation methods and costs. The marketing group must work with logistics to incorporate a supply chain perspective into packaging designs and trade-offs.

What Information Technology Needs to Know

1. *Impact to hardware and software requirements*—Any increase in production capacity may require change. This could be software upgrades or equipment purchases for both business and production operations. The IT group needs to know what information or communication technologies other functional areas will require for them to support this new product launch.

2. *Budget*—How much money is available for any IT upgrades that may be needed? Once IT knows what's required, they have to find a way to stay within the budget proposed by the finance department or discuss the situation with them if it's not sufficient.

Obviously, getting a six-pack of D2 Ultra into your hands will require a lot of up-front collaboration inside the brewery.

External Collaboration

Because internal collaboration efforts may not be monitored or rewarded, there might be less incentive for individuals inside a firm to work closely together than there is for collaboration outside the boundaries of the firm. One big incentive is financial reward. By working together, manufacturers, suppliers, and customers can produce better value and mutual rewards. Here are a few examples.

- The retail-ready packaging mentioned previously can be a source of benefit for manufacturers and retailers. By collaborating in the design of the packaging, the retailers can maximize the use of rack space, minimize the time required for stocking the items, and improve final customer access to the products in the store. The manufacturer gets the benefit of increased sales and a higher profile at the retail location.

- Retailers and manufacturers can also benefit by working together to segment retail sites by the sales volume and inventory turns for each product. This allows replenishment quantities and schedules to better match actual demand.

- Collaboration between manufacturers and their suppliers, when sourcing materials, has been around for quite a while. An OEM can lower the cost of parts it purchases from suppliers by contracting for the raw materials used to manufacture those parts. What the OEM does is negotiate a contract for the combined quantity of the same material that all its suppliers need. This gives the OEM the volume to get lower prices in the market. The lower priced material is then provided to suppliers who pass the savings on to the OEM.

Factors That Influence Collaboration

There are many factors that will assist or impede efforts to collaborate both internally and externally. The following are some of the most important:

1. *Goals*—When individual company functions or external suppliers are not aligned in support of the same goals, things go bad. Time lines, budgets, pricing, and cost management are just a few of the areas in which goals need to be jointly developed so every player on the team knows and agrees to his or her role in making it happen.

2. *Visibility*—A central feature of supply chain collaboration efforts has been a drive to provide all necessary members with visibility to information. The inability to predict and communicate demand patterns throughout the supply chain has caused problems in meeting customer expectations, utilizing manufacturing capacity, and managing inventory. (The result of these uncertainties produces great up and down swings in production and inventories. This is often called the "Bullwhip Effect" for the way it looks when represented on a graph.)

The assumption is that the more members who have access to demand data and supply requirements, the more certainty they will have about what is required and the easier it will be to efficiently synchronize supply chain activities.

In practice, this has proved costly and difficult. Such information sharing and coordinated planning cannot be done with all the members of a global network. Collaboration with only key members is a better approach. One challenge has been to identify who these members are and how to facilitate that collaboration. Technology has facilitated the capabilities available to provide visibility.

3. *Metrics* drive behavior internally and externally. An example is a brewer's performance expectations for product sales. Meeting the customers' yearning for a fine tasting, inexpensively priced beer is a great idea. But using a recipe that contains exotic additives and packaging the beer in fancy bottles would make low consumer pricing impractical. The sales group is measured on the revenue they produce. Supply management is measured on assuring supplies and controlling costs. Sales wants a low-priced, high-selling product, but to achieve that goal supply management is tasked with buying rare ingredients and specialty bottles at unrealistically low costs.

    These conflicts can happen whenever consumer pricing and product costs are not jointly planned up front. In Chapter 8, we'll go into greater detail with more examples of useful metrics and how they benefit everyone in the supply chain.

4. *Resources* necessary to collaborate internally and externally include financing, infrastructure, and personnel. Organizations throughout the supply chain often underestimate what it takes to collaborate. For example, putting the tasks required for supply chain collaboration on an already overstretched staff is self-defeating. Personnel up and down the chain of supply must be dedicated to the effort.

5. *Communication* frequency and clarity is a critical factor for successful collaboration both internally and externally. Infrastructure and technology support for communication is a must. Beyond the means of communication, support for open, frank dialogue among supply chain members helps to build trust.

6. *Information sharing* is an asset to everyone in a supply chain. Internally, functional areas need to get support for performance metrics that encourage dialogue and cooperation. Externally, the challenges are more difficult.

The interrelationships that suppliers may have with competitors can limit their willingness to disclose some information. For example, discussions about proprietary processes for competitive products would understandably be off-limits. Collaborating on production schedules and quantities should be a legitimate expectation. But openness about issues such as a supplier's cost structure will require trust. *Supplier relationship management* (SRM) initiatives, such as those used by Honda and Toyota, can help build that trust (as we'll see in Chapter 4).

7. *Trust* is not a concern when we are certain of how someone will act or respond to a situation. Trust becomes most valuable when there is uncertainty. Supply chain collaboration becomes easier when the parties can trust the ethics, the fairness, and the truthfulness of those with whom they work—both internally and externally.

8. *Equity and fairness* are assessments all people make. Negative judgments about fairness can cloud a relationship by reducing trust and communication. For instance, supply chain collaboration activities require time, effort, and resource commitments. But the outcomes are often unpredictable. Each party will want to see that those commitments have equitable returns.

Summary

Supply chain collaboration is widely discussed but difficult to do. Supply chain members must understand the challenges it presents and plan accordingly. Getting internal cooperation is the first place to start. Breaking down the barriers—such as those that arise from conflicts over performance expectations or a culture that rewards individual outcomes over collective achievements regardless of the methods used—is a great beginning.

Collaboration ranges from modest efforts, such as inventory management programs, to large scale integrated manufacturing and distribution planning systems. The resources required are consistent with the size and complexity of the methods employed. Not every external member in the chain is a candidate for collaboration. The effort required for collaboration initiatives must produce results. Choosing partners indiscriminately can be costly. Strategic planning, supply relationship management, and risk management must all factor into decisions regarding with whom to collaborate. Each of these topics will be discussed in subsequent chapters.

QUIZ

1. _____ among supply chain members can create competitive advantage.
   A. Collaboration
   B. Social awareness
   C. Competition
   D. Confrontations

2. _____ means that each party stands to gain something from collaboration.
   A. "Collectively"
   B. "Mutually beneficial"
   C. "Self-serving"
   D. "Benchmarks"

3. A supply chain has both internal and external _____
   A. stockholders.
   B. members.
   C. competitors.
   D. weather.

4. Methods such as *efficient consumer response* (ECR) are _____
   A. used by farmers.
   B. large in scale and complexity.
   C. very clearly understood.
   D. under government rules.

5. Supply chain collaboration is _____
   A. easy.
   B. nonproductive.
   C. challenging.
   D. a software package.

6. _____ must profitably identify, forecast, and satisfy customers' needs.
   A. Accounting
   B. The CEO
   C. Production
   D. Marketing

7. The primary function of _____ is to obtain external resources required by a firm.
   A. corporate officers
   B. supply management
   C. finance
   D. production

8. Tier 1 suppliers provide parts and materials directly to the _____
   A. competitors.
   B. retailers.
   C. warehouse.
   D. OEM.

9. The _____ department is the group that manages the firm's money.
   A. human resources
   B. finance
   C. inventory control
   D. marketing

10. The basic function of _____ is moving and storing products and materials.
    A. sales
    B. suppliers
    C. logistics
    D. labor

11. A manufacturer _____ inputs to create a product.
    A. transforms
    B. disassembles
    C. sells
    D. transports

12. A _____ is a middleman between the manufacturer and the retailer.
    A. wholesaler
    B. support
    C. freight carrier
    D. retail store

13. _____ provide an incentive for external supply chain collaboration.
    A. Threats
    B. Regulations
    C. Financial rewards
    D. Products

14. Poorly designed departmental performance metrics may _____
    A. be illegal.
    B. discourage collaboration.
    C. cause illness.
    D. be okay.

15. Visibility to _____ across the supply chain helps with efforts to collaborate.
    A. dividend payments
    B. weather patterns
    C. information
    D. profit margins

chapter 3

Supply Chain Strategies and Planning

The focus of this chapter is strategy, and strategy starts with customers. Business organizations exist to meet the needs and wants of customers. Whatever a firm provides, customers must want it and be willing to pay for it. Plan the work and work the plan: that's the essence of how to create a customer-focused strategy and implement it.

CHAPTER OBJECTIVES

In this chapter, you will learn

- What the levels of decision making in an organization are.
- What some of the tools to use in strategy development are.
- What a supply chain strategy is and how it is linked to business strategy.
- What some common supply chain strategies in use today are.
- Why strategic sourcing is important and how it is done.

Supply chain management (SCM) is a boundary-spanning activity that occurs both internally and externally. Therefore, merging the development of business and supply chain strategies not only makes sense, but is also critical. Bringing supply chain decisions into senior executives' planning processes ensures that the sort of internal collaboration required is directed from the highest echelons of an organization. This means that resources are dedicated to the supply chain and performance measures are chosen that support it.

Two areas of particular importance for decision makers are supply management and logistics strategies. Supply management strategy will be reviewed here, and topics specific to logistics will be covered in Chapter 6. In this chapter, we will look at organizational decision-making processes and identify supply chain management's place within them. We'll cover some common tools for decision making and how they are applicable to both the high-level business strategy and the supply chain strategy that supports it.

Levels of Decision Making

In any organization, there are three levels of decision making: *strategic, tactical,* and *operational*. A business strategy is a plan created at the top level of the decision-making processes. Decisions regarding supply chain strategies can be made at the strategic level or the tactical level to support the higher-level business strategy. Operational decisions are made daily in getting the job done. As illustrated in Figure 3-1, these levels of decision making can be represented as three segments of a pyramid according to the different attributes of each type of decision.

- *Strategic decisions* are about the long-term direction of the organization and flow down from the organization's values and mission. Strategic planning starts with the customer. What does the firm do to deliver value to the customer? Answering this question requires a firm to scan its environment and seek developing patterns and trends that may have an impact on the business. It includes risk analysis planning for any new initiatives, such as markets to be served and policies to be enacted. Senior management must also decide how resources will be allocated to fund any initiatives.

  Example—A strategic decision could be to leverage the organization's expertise by entering a new market with different products.

- *Tactical decisions* identify the methods by which the upper level strategic objectives will be carried out. These decisions are medium term and more

FIGURE 3-1 · Decision-making levels.

flexible in response to changing circumstances. They include allocating available resources and identifying any risks that may prevent meeting objectives.

Example—In support of an executive decision to enter a new market, managers must plan the methods by which it can be done. Issues such as product development, marketing plans, supplier sourcing, and supply chain design need to be addressed.

- *Operational decisions* involve the day-to-day aspects of running the business. These are the everyday tasks and interactions that take place to implement the methods chosen for achieving the goals of the business plan.

Example—These operations would include tasks that are required to fulfill the tactical plans managers have created to support the executive strategy. In the example of a new product introduction, tasks such as meeting requirements, scheduling production, purchasing materials, and planning transportation should be implemented.

Decision-Making Tools and Techniques

When any organization is trying to develop a strategy, it helps to have a framework for how to go about it. There are a variety of tools and techniques available for developing strategies. Because no single method can get at all the questions that need answers, most of the time a combination of techniques is used. These tools don't provide specific answers, but they do offer a structure for finding them. Three of the most common ones are: *SWOT analysis*, *PEST analysis*, and *value chain analysis*.

SWOT Analysis

SWOT is an acronym for strengths, weaknesses, opportunities, and threats. The first two sets of factors are internal to the organization, and the last two are external.

- SWOT analysis is a useful tool for gathering and analyzing information, but it's also a subjective tool. So it's best used in combination with other analysis techniques.

- When done well, a SWOT analysis can help an organization maximize the value of its strengths and opportunities while overcoming internal weaknesses and minimizing external threats.

The chart in Table 3-1 illustrates the sort of questions that would be included in each quadrant of a typical SWOT diagram used at the strategic level

TABLE 3-1 Basic SWOT Analysis Chart

Strengths	Opportunities
Strengths are the tangible or intangible factors that aid the firm in fulfilling its mission. Questions: -- What is the firm's competitive advantage? -- What superior capabilities, brand recognition, or financial or intellectual resources does it have? -- What does it do that is unique among its competitors? -- What do the consumer and supplier markets view as the firm's strengths?	Opportunities may be discovered in markets, competition, government, and technology. Questions: -- What market opportunities exist now? -- What new market opportunities are coming? -- What are competitors' weaknesses? -- Is there any new potential for exporting or importing? -- What political, economic, social, or technological changes will create opportunities? (PEST)
Weaknesses	**Threats**
Weaknesses are the factors that keep the firm from fulfilling its mission. Questions: -- What do other firms do better? -- What does not add value in the firm's operations? -- What do consumers and suppliers view as the firm's weaknesses? -- What does the firm lack in terms of financial, equipment, or personnel resources?	Threats include all the possible risks that exist in the external environment. Questions: -- What threats might current or future competitors bring? -- What political, economic, social, or technological changes pose threats? (PEST) -- What changes may there be in the employment market? -- What climate changes are expected?

of planning. Each SWOT analysis must address external factors that are relevant to the subject of the analysis. For example, a supply chain analysis would also have different factors, such as transportation modes or carriers, technologies employed, and inventory management.

One critical question a SWOT analysis needs to answer is, "What is the firm's position in the supply chain?" Is it as a small player in a large, multitiered chain of supply, or does it dominate its supply chain? Few companies have the clout of Wal-Mart. A firm needs to be realistic about the power it has in order to get cooperation with other supply chain members. Knowing the firm's position and power will, in turn, influence the design of a supply chain strategy.

PEST Analysis

PEST stands for political, economic, social (and cultural), and technological factors. This acronym is frequently expanded to include other sets of influencing factors, such as legal and environmental (PESTLE or PESTEL). As seen in Figure 3-2, these are forces that are likely to have an impact on a firm and its operations. Like the SWOT analysis, a PEST template is a matrix of four quadrants. The importance of any one of the quadrants varies by industry and the nature of the firm.

Also like a SWOT analysis, the PEST matrix is used as a template to brainstorm ideas for each type of external factor. The questions raised may often be the same as or similar to those in the SWOT analysis. The focus of SWOT analysis is primarily on the business; the focus of PEST analysis is on external changes in trends, markets, resources, suppliers, competitors, and so on.

A process that engages both SWOT and PEST techniques can be useful when formulating a strategy because the two perspectives complement each

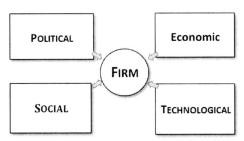

FIGURE 3-2 · Outside factors that affect a firm.

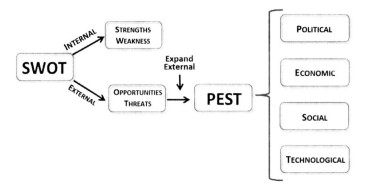

FIGURE 3-3 · SWOT & PEST analysis: a combined approach for strategic planning analysis.

other. The SWOT & PEST analysis chart in Figure 3-3 suggests how they can be combined in a practical framework for strategic analysis.

Value Chain Analysis

Next we look at value chain analysis. Who are the customers? Just about all firms have many of them. In addition, from a supply chain perspective there are both "customers" and "consumers," as noted in Chapter 1. From suppliers to final consumer, each transaction between the members of that chain of supply involves the exchange of goods and money—an exchange of value. As explained in Chapter 1, what customers value is highly subjective, but it's also very important to the design of a supply chain strategy. What are customers' top priorities? Is getting their products quickly the top priority? Is it the cheapest prices? Is it the latest fashion? Do they want the highest quality and are they willing to pay for it? That is the key. Knowing who the customers are and what they value unlocks the door to supply chain design possibilities that are based on customer-perceived benefits.

Value chain analysis starts with the premise that an organization is supposed to add value for its customers. But the customer also needs to see that value proposition, and firms need strategies to support it. Capital One offers a "No Hassles Rewards card" and built a customer interface system to support it. Wal-Mart offers "Always low prices" and created a huge, efficient supply chain network to ensure the supply of low-priced goods. To begin to understand how it adds value, a firm must first understand the characteristics of its market. Once the benchmarks for value have been established, a firm can move on to value chain analysis. Value chain analysis helps answer the following questions:

1. What value is the organization creating for customers?

2. In what ways are the activities that are being done in the supply chain contributing to that value?

As discussed in Chapter 1, Michael Porter showed that firms could differentiate themselves by providing better value to customers. (See Figure 3-4.)

Value chain analysis identifies all interconnected linkages in the network of supply chain activities. Whatever is being done will add cost, so it must also add value from the customer's perspective or it is "waste." Once identified, areas of costs can be reviewed for change. These changes might include:

- Streamlining activities or eliminating those that are non-value-adding by:
  - Shipping directly to stores instead of through warehouses; collaborating with retail operations to eliminate the transaction costs of warehousing
  - Using cross docking in warehouse operations, that is, breaking down incoming shipments and immediately consolidating them into outgoing shipments

- Reducing the complexity of processes and tasks by:
  - Revising and electronically automating processes, such as eliminating paperwork for purchase orders, invoices, and customer order processing
  - Investing in communication and automation technologies, such as bar codes, RFID, and ERP systems, that will all help to find, track, and deliver products

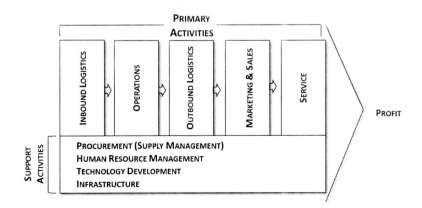

FIGURE 3-4 · Value chain.

The value chain analysis process begins by first separating the firm's internal functions into primary and support activities, as illustrated by Figure 3-4. Primary activities are those directly associated with production; support activities are those sustaining the overall capabilities of the organization.

Primary Activities:

- Inbound logistics includes everything associated with getting raw materials and parts from suppliers to the point of use.

- Marketing and sales incorporate all the activities that must be performed to profitably identify, forecast, and satisfy customers' needs and wants.

- Operations consist of everything that it takes to create products or services.

- Outbound logistics includes all the activities required to bring the product to the customer or engage the customer to provide a service.

- Service involves anything necessary to provide the customer with pre- or post-sales assistance, such as installation, warranty work, or repairs.

Support Activities

- Supply management must ensure the supply of all the materials, parts, and services required by the organization.

- Human resource management is associated with the recruitment, retention, and training of company personnel.

- Technology development is involved with research, development, and deployment of innovative technologies that support the activities of the value chain.

- Firm infrastructure includes functions, such as legal, financial, and other planning and control systems.

Keys to Doing a Value Chain Analysis

Some keys for conducting a value chain analysis include the following:

1. Know what the organization's core competency is:
   - It is the reason the organization exists. It must do this to meet customer needs and wants.
   - It must provide a customer-perceived benefit. If the customers don't think it's valuable, why do it?

- It's something competitors cannot easily imitate. A competency that any competitor can imitate may be purchased from a third party (outsourced). This will allow the allocation of organizational resources to things that are core related.

- It's a competency that can be maintained over time.

2. Segment internal activities into primary and support categories.

3. Identify what those activities do and how that adds value.

4. Look for opportunities to improve the value added by each.

5. Create strategies that maximize the value-adding potential of activities, which can help create a competitive advantage.

What each of these three tools—SWOT, PEST, and value chain analysis—offers is a process for collecting, categorizing, and evaluating information so that strategies are based on data and analysis and not on "gut feelings." The next section begins with some specific considerations in choosing a supply chain strategy and what some of the common types of strategies are.

Supply Chain Strategy

Supply chain strategies must support the organization's overall business strategy, and that is the context in which they should be created. There is no one right business strategy, and there is no one right supply chain strategy. The answer to both is always, "it depends." The industry sector in which the firm operates is a prime example of a factor that prevents a "one-size-fits-all" strategy. A strategy that works well for *consumer packaged goods* (CPG) companies, such as Coca Cola and Procter & Gamble, will not necessarily work for automobile companies like Toyota or farm equipment manufacturers like John Deere.

One of the challenges of creating supply chain strategies is the fact that developing one requires cross-functional collaboration among all the internal supply chain members. As part of the organization-wide strategy and planning processes illustrated previously, each functional area within the company will create a separate plan for themselves. In many firms, supply chain management is a concept but is no one's dedicated responsibility. Those with primary responsibility for key supply chain processes, marketing, supply management, finance, production, logistics, and *information technology* (IT), must develop their individual plans with supply chain needs in mind. Performance expectations and metrics are factors that were mentioned before as either impediments to internal collaboration or facilitators of it. Chapter 8 covers the topic of supply chain metrics and how it relates to collaboration.

In their book, *Supply Chain Management* (2013), Sunil Chopra and Peter Meindl, propose that supply chain strategy development is done in the first of a three-phase decision-making process: (1) supply chain strategy or design, (2) supply chain planning, and (3) supply chain operations. Here is a summary of the three phases and the decisions that must be made in each one.

1. *Supply chain strategy or design*—This phase includes decisions about the long-term structure of the firm's supply chain. These decisions are not easily or inexpensively reversed so they must anticipate market changes:
   - Supply chain configuration
   - Resource allocations
   - Processes performed at each stage (such as the movement from material supplier to manufacturer)
   - Outsourcing of supply chain functions versus performing them internally
   - Location and capacities of production and warehouse facilities
   - Products to be manufactured or stored at various locations
   - Modes of transportation to be made available
   - Information technologies to be used

2. *Supply chain planning*—These are midterm decisions for one year or less. Firms estimate a forecast for the year ahead in different markets and create a plan that will work within the constraints and flexibility offered by the supply chain configuration established in phase one. Uncertainties, such as currency valuation, demand changes, and competition, must also be addressed in this phase. Decisions in this phase need to be made about the following:
   - Locations that will supply each market
   - Subcontracting of manufacturing
   - Inventory and operating policies
   - Timing and size of marketing promotions

3. *Supply chain operations*—These are often real-time decisions made daily about how best to accommodate customer orders and include tasks, such as allocating inventory or production to individual orders, setting an order fill date, and arranging for shipment.

Sales and Operations Planning

One area of tactical decision making related to the second phase of Chopra and Meindl's process is very important: *Sales and Operations Planning* (S&OP). S&OP is a decision-making process necessary to balance demand and supply. An imbalance between supply and demand can be very costly. It can result in either out-of-stock or excess inventory situations at points in the chain of supply. Not having the product where and when it is needed results in lost sales revenue and frustrates customers. Having too much inventory anywhere in the chain adds waste.

In the S&OP process, executive-level management meets regularly to review forecasts for demand and supply and the possible implications for the firm's finances. Whenever there appear to be imbalances in these three areas, alternatives and options are proposed to rebalance them. The goal is to ensure that tactical planning and the daily operational activities that support it are consistent with the overall business plan. To accomplish that end, executives discuss key areas of importance, such as the following:

- Demand and revenue expectations
- Production plans
- Cost of sales projections
- Inventory locations and quantities

Issues of Strategic Importance

To be effective, a supply chain strategy needs to set the stage for making many crucial decisions. Choices must be made about the issues on the following list, which supplement those identified by Chopra and Meindl.

- *Supply chain network*—Decisions regarding the number, location, and size of warehousing, distribution centers, and facilities
- *Logistics network*—The use of third-party logistics firms, choice of transportation mode, and cross-docking methods. (These will be further explained in Chapter 6.)
- *Supply management (sourcing and procurement) strategy*—Decisions regarding the number, location, size and type of suppliers, and the type of supplier relationships must be supportive of and integrated into the supply chain strategy.

- *Relationships with other members of the supply chain*—The choice of which distributors, wholesalers, and retailers to use.
- *Communication and technology networks*—Decisions about which technologies will be employed and how they will be integrated, including technological enablers, such as compatible software, RFID, and information and financial sharing capabilities.

The issues and factors outlined above demonstrate that the supply chain strategy chosen by a firm is dependent upon many factors. Perhaps the most important point is that a strategy must support the way in which the firm has chosen to differentiate itself in the market. This may require segmenting the market and having more than one supply chain strategy to support each segment.

Types of Supply Chain Strategies

Based upon the needs of a market segment, a firm may choose to focus its strategy on one (or more) supply chain capabilities, such as speed, efficiency, agility, or flexibility. These basic strategies are described next, along with the industries they best fit and their primary objectives.

Speed

A speed strategy is particularly important for industries with a high velocity of product innovation and short product life cycles. They need to design the product, manufacture it, and get it to fickle customers ahead of the competition. Companies that make consumer electronic and communication products are most suited for this strategy.

Objectives for this strategy include:

- Close collaboration with offshore assembly plants
- Manufacture of products with predictable demand in continuous flow facilities in order to maximize efficiencies and reduce costs
- Use of contract manufacturing on an as-needed basis in order to accommodate both seasonal fluctuations in demand and products with low sales volume
- Use of all available analytics tools in order to anticipate demand and conduct sales forecasting and planning
- Collaboration among design engineers, supply management, and suppliers in order to standardize parts and assembly across the product line

Efficiency

Producers of commodities such as steel and paper have a heavy investment in capital equipment. They also operate in a market where price competition is fierce. For them, a supply chain focused on efficiency provides the best means of asset utilization and cost control. Objectives for this strategy are the following:

- Use of customer segmentation to identify those with whom supply chain collaboration efforts would be beneficial
- Reduction in the complexity of the product mix in order to minimize low-volume products with unstable demand
- Flexibility in outbound transportation in order to accommodate fluctuations in the volume of orders
- Close attention to S&OP in order to maximize forecast accuracy and schedule production most efficiently
- Provision of sufficient storage capacity to accommodate seasonal variability in demand when appropriate

Agility

An agile supply chain is one that can quickly adapt to change. Along with make-to-order companies, the firms that will use this approach are those that compete where time to market is critical or that have unpredictable product demand patterns. Objectives for this strategy are the following:

- Close collaboration with domestic and offshore suppliers
- Commonality of product platforms and components
- Tight inventory management
- Visibility to real-time sales and transportation information

Flexibility

Flexible supply chain designs offer the opportunity to react to changing demand in manufacturing or to provide time-sensitive response in the service sector. High demand variability for their product or services is a characteristic of firms using this approach.

A manufacturer could have multiple facilities and each one could produce a variety of the same products. This would allow shifting production volumes among the different plants depending on demand. Service firms that promise a quick response require a strategy for tapping reserves of labor when necessary

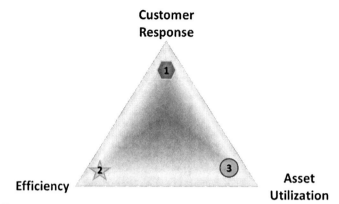

Adapted from: L Lapide "The Operational Performance Triangles" Supply Chain Management Review November 2008

FIGURE 3-5 • Operational performance triangle.

and maintaining the equipment and supplies needed to respond. Objectives for this strategy are the following:

- Supply chain collaboration and *supply relationship management* (SRM)
- The use of analytical tools to anticipate demand fluctuations

A way to help visualize the proper application of strategies is a variation of Dr. Larry Lapide's "Operational Performance Triangle," as shown in Figure 3-5. (This concept will be discussed further in Chapter 8.) Below is a brief description of the three operational objectives shown in Lapide's Triangle.

1. In the Lapide model, a focus on customer response is characterized by high margin and short life-cycle products as evident in firms, such as pharmaceutical, fashion apparel, and entertainment.

2. Efficiency is an important objective for food and beverage companies, for staples in retail companies, and for industrial supply companies. These companies offer mature products with low margins.

3. Capital intensive industries, like semiconductor fabrication, petrochemical, and commodities (steel, paper, or coal), would best be served by focusing on asset utilization (which can also be a measure of efficiency).

Sustaining a Competitive Advantage

Like any organism, firms and their supply chains must adapt to survive and flourish. That means supply chain strategy must also be flexible and adaptive.

Companies such as Wal-Mart in the retail sector and Dell in electronics have used supply chain management to their competitive advantage. However, as more retailers have succeeded in mimicking Wal-Mart's supply chain operations, it has become less of a differentiating advantage for them. Dell's strategy of customer-direct selling was innovative and set it apart from other computer manufacturers in the 1990s. As the market for computers matured and competitors adopted some of Dell's methods, it had to modify its supply chain strategies to include retail distribution.

In the past, few firms focused on supply chain management strategy as a way to differentiate themselves. Finding and driving out costs was the primary objective. Today, there is greater recognition that supply chain management offers support for more options than just cost reduction. To maximize their advantage, some organizations are trying to merge the various options for strategies and thereby gain all the benefits of each one. This may be difficult to do since certain objectives in each strategy seem incompatible. The success of overlapping strategies is not yet proven. However, there is reason to be optimistic that separate supply chain strategies for different customer segments can be managed by one firm. That seems logical as long as the costs of doing so do not outweigh the value of benefits it provides.

Strategic Sourcing

The sourcing and supply management function is one of the most important elements of supply chain management. Supply management assures that purchased materials and services required by the organization are available when needed. Sourcing is a process within supply management that deals with supplier selection and management. Chapter 4 offers a number of ways in which the supply management function contributes to excellence in supply chain management. The focus here is on the importance and development of a strategic sourcing process, which is a big issue for some firms because they lack a defined process for selecting and managing suppliers.

Not having a specific process in place leads to the misallocation of resources necessary to manage purchases from outside suppliers. It also affects the potential of supply chain activity if poor supplier selections are made.

Strategic Sourcing Defined

Strategic sourcing provides great opportunities to increase profitability and improve supply chain performance. It is a rigorous, systematic process by which an organization analyzes its expenditures, evaluates both internal and external influences, and determines the appropriate sourcing methods necessary to support overall organizational goals. Strategic sourcing decisions include the following:

- Number and location of suppliers
- Types of relationships
- Length of agreements
- Systems and processes

A firm must focus resources on activities such as supplier management and away from non-value-adding activity such as processing requisitions for low dollar purchases. One way to do that is to have a strategy for cost-effectively buying everything a firm requires. The goal of strategic sourcing is to reduce cost, maximize the firm's performance, and fulfill customer needs while mitigating risks. The primary steps needed to accomplish this include the analysis of the organization's expenditures, segmentation of that spending into categories, and creating supply management strategies for each category.

Analysis Of Organizational Spending

An analysis of the organization's current spending is absolutely necessary. It includes both traditional areas of responsibility for supply managers, such as direct materials and maintenance supplies along with nontraditional areas, such as travel and professional services. In addition to how much is purchased by category and supplier as shown in Figure 3-6, this analysis is expected to answer questions such as:

- What is purchased?
- From whom are the purchases made?
- When, how, and by whom are purchases made?

Once all the spend information is assembled and categorized, some opportunities for improvement will become immediately evident. For example, as illustrated in Figure 3-6, there may be too many suppliers being used or too many very similar parts being purchased. By acting to make changes, companies can begin to see the rewards of the strategic sourcing process while it is still

Identify expenditures by:

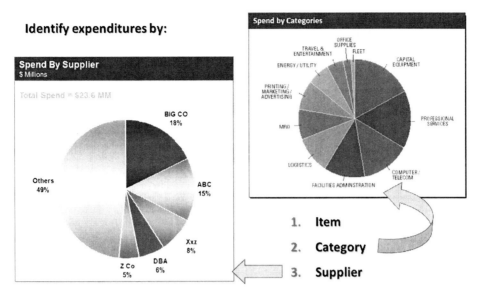

FIGURE 3-6 · Results of the spend analysis.

being conducted. The next step is to segment the spending according to its characteristics.

Segment the Organizational Spend

By using *quadrant analysis* (or *portfolio analysis* as it may be called), the spending is segmented into four categories such as those illustrated in Figure 3-8. These quadrants are developed by plotting the relative risk associated with a type of purchase and the relative value that the purchase has for the organiza-

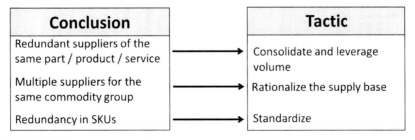

FIGURE 3-7 · Opportunities for Improvement.

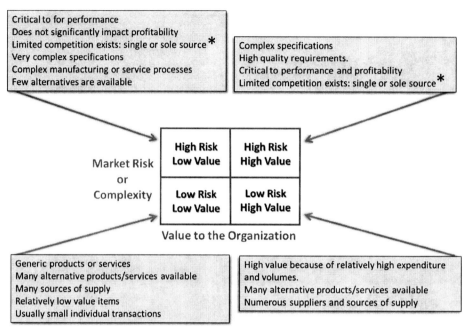

FIGURE 3-8 · Quadrant analysis: four categories of spending.

tion. Characteristics that define what purchases go where are then created and plotted in each quadrant. The actual items that go into each category will vary according to what the firm purchases.

Develop Strategies for Each Category

Once the analysis is complete, the organization can determine how best to manage the buys in each category. The lists below show several of the common ways this is done.

High Risk–Low Value

- Use negotiated agreements.
- Use standard agreements with performance incentives.
- Use long-term agreements (life of product).
- Create collaborative relationships.

- Engage in continuous improvement.
- Take action to move to another quadrant.

High Risk–High Value

- Use supplier alliances.
- Encourage collaboration in SCM.
- Encourage collaboration in technologies.
- Use open-book pricing.
- Use cost analysis.
- Negotiate agreements.
- Ensure organizational alignment in strategies.
- Build supplier relationships.

Low Risk–Low Value

- Standardize, consolidate, and use commercial specifications.
- Negotiate competitively bid agreements.
- Use blanket agreements.
- Allow users to release orders.
- Use electronic catalogues and ordering.
- Use purchasing cards (credit cards).
- Remove supply management personnel from order processing.

Low Risk–High Value

- Negotiate competitively bid agreements.
- Negotiate value-added services.
- Negotiate improvement clauses.
- Use master agreements with release mechanisms.
- Allow for flexibility in response to market changes.
- Base terms on market conditions and performance.
- Use transaction-reducing, order-release mechanisms.

Once this part of the process is complete, supply managers have the ability to select the most efficient and effective way for purchases to be made. For example, by taking all "low-low" buys and setting up contracts that cover many products, the buyer can get better pricing and service through competition. Office supplies are one good example of how this is done. A contract is negotiated with an office supply distributor, and the items to be purchased are put into an online catalogue. Then it's possible for the users to point and click to make a purchase. It eliminates paperwork and frees up buyers' time. Correspondingly, buyers now have more time to engage in strategic activities with the suppliers from whom they purchase items in the "high-high" quadrant.

Characteristics of Integrated Supply Management

Organizations that have done strategic sourcing well have gotten great benefit from it. Putting effort where it has the best chance to add value is what the process achieves. However, strategic sourcing initiatives alone cannot maximize the value of supply management. The strategy must be tightly aligned and integrated with other internal supply chain related functions. Some of the characteristics of the supply management groups that have made it happen include the following:

1. All internal supply chain management functions are integrated.
2. Suppliers are chosen strategically.
3. Common goals exist for both the buying organization and the suppliers.
4. Proper supplier relationships are in place.
5. Integrative performance metrics are in place.
6. Cost management tools are actively used.
7. Suppliers are actively engaged in all product or services development.
8. Redundant, inefficient processes are aggressively eliminated.
9. Appropriate technological enablers are integrated.
10. SRM is ongoing.

Summary

Supply chain management strategies must support the overall business strategy and can help differentiate a firm from its competition. However, to maximize the benefits achieved, the needs of the supply chain in meeting customer demands must be reflected at all levels of the decision-making process. The greatest impact comes from executive-level awareness of and commitments to supply chain excellence. This executive-level involvement helps ensure that supply chain strategies are woven into the business strategy and that resources are committed to it.

There is no one right supply chain strategy. The most effective ones are those that support what customers value. Time to market, speed of delivery, prices, and convenience are valued differently among customer groups. The most effective strategies are those in which a firm clearly understands the needs and wants of key customer segments and creates a supply chain strategy to meet them.

QUIZ

1. In any organization there are _____ levels of decision making.
    A. six
    B. two
    C. three
    D. one

2. Strategic decisions are about the _____ direction of the organization.
    A. short-term
    B. current
    C. long-term
    D. market

3. Tactical decisions identify the methods needed to meet _____ objectives.
    A. upper-level strategic
    B. daily operational
    C. functional
    D. new product

4. SWOT is an acronym for strengths, weaknesses, _____, and threats.
    A. options
    B. opportunities
    C. opinions
    D. outcomes

5. PEST stands for political, economic, social, and _____ factors.
    A. time
    B. transition
    C. technological
    D. transportation

6. The purpose of value chain analysis is to identify how an organization can pro-vide value for its ____
    A. employees.
    B. suppliers.
    C. customers.
    D. creditors.

7. A strategy that works well for *consumer packaged goods* (CPG) companies _____ for other companies.
    A. is probably best
    B. will not necessarily work

C. is easy to implement

D. is hard to do

8. Developing supply chain strategies requires _____ among all the internal supply chain members.

A. complete agreement

B. short meetings

C. personal interest

D. cross-functional collaboration

9. Some keys to doing a value chain analysis include knowing what the organization's _____ is.

A. core competency

B. financial situation

C. stock price

D. revenue

10. Supply chain strategies must support the _____

A. organization's overall business strategy.

B. suppliers' income.

C. short-term goals.

D. production plans.

11. A firm may choose to focus its strategy on supply chain capabilities, such as _____, efficiency, agility, or flexibility.

A. spending

B. location

C. speed

D. production

12. S&OP is a decision-making process necessary to balance _____

A. demand and supply.

B. market expectations.

C. supplier revenue.

D. debt and income.

13. Important factors that influence the choice of a supply chain strategy include the _____ in which the firm exists, the market for products, variability of demand, and product life cycle.

A. location

B. nation

C. industry

D. culture

14. An important element in a strategic sourcing process includes_____
    A. productive meetings.
    B. new performance metrics.
    C. an analysis of expenditures.
    D. daily conversations.

15. A sourcing strategy must balance the _____ of different types of purchases.
    A. seasonality
    B. employees' opinions
    C. relative risk and relative value
    D. timing

chapter 4

Sourcing and Supply Management

The primary function of supply management is to purchase all the external resources necessary to support a firm's activities. *Sourcing* is part of a supply management process used to identify and select potential suppliers. In this chapter, we will highlight four essential ways that supply management supports supply chain network performance and enhances its value to customers: (1) supplier management, (2) negotiation and contracting, (3) cost control, and (4) innovation and *new product development* (NPD).

CHAPTER OBJECTIVES

In this chapter, you will learn

- How global sourcing has influenced supplier management practices.
- How suppliers are selected.
- What *supplier relationship management* (SRM) is.
- Supply management's role in make-versus-buy and outsourcing decisions.
- How buyer-supplier negotiations are conducted.
- Supply management's contribution to cost control.
- How supply management helps propel innovation and speed new product development.

Supplier Management

The globalization of production, the opening of international markets for goods and services, the increased pressure for cost management, and issues surrounding resource availability have all contributed to moving the emphasis in businesses from price-driven, tactical buying to strategic supply management. The most significant factor that has influenced this change is the development of complex global supplier networks. Interdependence among the members of these networks brings risks and challenges that need to be managed. Supply management is the system best suited to do it.

An excellent supply base is a major asset to any firm—but it doesn't just happen. Decisions must be made about which suppliers to use, when to use a supplier or to do something internally (make versus buy), where the best location in the world is for sourcing those suppliers, and then how to manage them. An explanation of the following four topics will show how supply management personnel answer all of those questions:

1. Supplier selection
2. Make-versus-buy and outsourcing decisions
3. Global sourcing
4. *Supplier relationship management* (SRM)

Supplier Selection

The first step in supplier management is selecting the right suppliers. Suppliers are critical to effective supply chain management. They are the members of the chain that provide all the resources necessary to create and move products to customers. The method a firm uses to identify, evaluate, qualify, select, and manage suppliers is critical. The flow chart in Figure 4-1 provides a visual representation of a way by which suppliers are moved from the stage of *identification* to that of *supplier approval* through a rigorous process.

Process Steps

These 8 steps are essential to the supplier selection process:

Step 1—The first step in the process is the development of a supply management strategy. The sourcing strategy (outlined in Chapter 3) provides the guidelines for supplier selection.

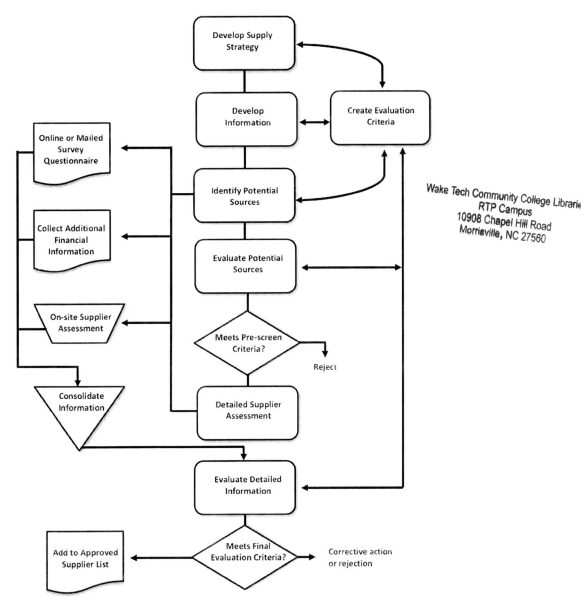

FIGURE 4-1 · Supplier selection process flowchart.

Step 2—As illustrated, the preliminary selection criteria may be modified. For example, if the strategy involves locating suppliers within a short distance of the buyer's facility and none exist, the criteria will need to be changed.

Step 3—The process of locating potential suppliers may begin with recommendations from colleagues or outside associates. It might also include information gathered from trade shows or publications. Today, the most common research tool is the Internet. Dedicated directories on the Internet, such as ThomasNet, WebstersOnline, or Kompass, are efficient search tools.

Steps 4 & 5—From the assembled preliminary information, suppliers are compared according to the selection criteria and appropriate potential ones are chosen.

Step 6—The process then continues with further in-depth investigation of the suppliers that made the first cut. This step would include a mailed or online *request for information* (RFI), the assembly of financial and other company-related information, and an on-site visit to evaluate the potential supplier's capabilities and quality assurance methods.

Steps 7 & 8—Once steps one through six are completed, a detailed assessment is made of all the information gathered. A supplier that meets all the required criteria would then be added to the Approved Supplier List. A supplier that doesn't meet the selection criteria in some small way may be asked to submit a corrective action plan that would bring them into compliance. Suppliers that are seriously noncompliant or do not wish to submit a corrective action plan are eliminated from the pool of potential sources.

Firms absolutely must control the supplier selection process. If everybody in the organization is allowed to choose suppliers without regard to the buying firm's strategic needs, there's really no benefit in having a sourcing strategy. Supply management is not alone in the universe of organizational stakeholders. However, to maximize the value the supplier base contributes to the supply chain, this function must be at the center of that decision-making process, as illustrated in Figure 4-2.

Once again, the process of internal collaboration among several departments is required. Stakeholders from manufacturing, engineering, production, distribution, *quality assurance* (QA), and finance should all contribute to the criteria for selection. Some of these personnel would contribute information to the evaluation process while others, such as engineering and QA, would be active participants in it.

Make-versus-Buy and Outsourcing Decisions

The choice of whether to do something internally or have an outside firm do it is referred to as a make-versus-buy decision. The term *outsourcing* is frequently applied to any type of activity that was or could be performed internally but is done by an outside provider instead. In other words, any make-versus-buy decision that results in contracting with an outside provider is called outsourcing. Outsourcing can be done with domestic U.S. firms or with companies in other countries (*offshore outsourcing*).

There are many reasons why a firm may want to go outside for the manufacture of products or for service providers, including the following:

- In-house expertise to do or create what is needed is lacking.
- Shifting the job to a supplier with better capabilities reduces company risk.
- A sole source is the only one capable of providing a product or service.
- Technology is unavailable in-house.
- Temporary requirements do not justify doing it inside.
- Customers have required the use of specific service providers.
- Total cost is improved because an outside provider is more efficient and effective.
- A company's core competencies do not include doing this activity.
- The lead time available is too short to staff or tool up to do it inside.

FIGURE 4-2 • Stakeholders in the supplier selection process.

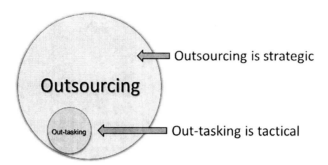

FIGURE 4-3 • Outsourcing versus out-tasking.

There is a difference between *out-tasking* and outsourcing. Out-tasking is done for something relatively minor, whereas outsourcing is a strategic decision. As shown in Figure 4-3, out-tasking decisions may be seen as a subset of outsourcing. However, such decisions rarely have the sort of strategic impact that the outsourcing of an entire company function or process would have.

Still Struggling

Consider these situations. Suppose you are the buyer for a facilities management department in a large corporate office complex located near Chicago. Here are two different scenarios.

1. One day the boss comes in and tells you that the snowplow has to be replaced, so this year he wants to outsource snow removal in all the parking lots. You are tasked with finding a snow removal service provider and contracting for its services.

   Questions:

   Is this a strategic decision? Does it involve risk, dislocation of employees, high cost, or a limited pool of available suppliers? No.

   Can the company recover quickly if this service provider does not perform? Yes.

2. One day the boss comes in and tells you he got a call from the company president, who told him the officer group decided to outsource all facilities management services in order to save money. Your job is to help him find a company to take over all maintenance for the grounds, buildings, HVAC systems, plumbing, electrical, and so on.

Questions:

Is this a strategic decision? Does it involve risk, dislocation of employees, high cost, or a limited pool of available suppliers? Yes.

Can the company recover quickly if this service provider does not perform? No.

The situation in scenario 1 didn't create a costly or risky decision. There are many local firms available to provide snow removal services. Source selection should be relatively quick and easy. If one service provider fails to meet expectations, another can be readily found. It's a low-cost, easily recoverable decision.

In scenario 2, the situation is quite different. Company executives have decided to turn over the maintenance and general upkeep of what is surely a multimillion-dollar facility to an outside provider. Source selection will not be that easy; it will take time and require considerable expertise in completing the acquisition process, leading to a well-negotiated and beneficially structured contract. Once done, this will not be a decision from which the company can easily recover and bring the work back inside. All the maintenance equipment will have been sold. Quite likely several personnel will have moved on to other employment.

1. Scenario 1 was out-tasking. An outside provider would be hired to perform just one of many tasks that are part of facilities management.

2. Scenario 2 is outsourcing. An entire company function is being eliminated, and the care of a multimillion-dollar company asset will now be an outside firm's responsibility.

The differences are important to consider. Supply management's expertise is useful in the first scenario and absolutely critical in the second.

Supply management can help assess the strategic implications of an outsourcing decision and engage in supplier selection, contracting, and negotiation. The most important documents in this process will be the *request for proposal* (RFP) and a negotiated *statement of work* (SOW).

Global Sourcing

Where in the world to source suppliers? As global sourcing has become more important over the past two decades, supply management's role has gotten more complex and challenging. If it's difficult to manage suppliers locally, it's even harder when the buying and supplying firms are thousands of miles apart.

Sourcing typically refers to the process by which a firm identifies and selects sources of supply for the products and services it requires. (In the *supply-chain operations-reference* [SCOR] model, the term *sourcing* embraces all the activities associated with the purchasing process.) *Global sourcing* is the search for and selection of suppliers anywhere in the world. This type of supplier selection elevates the process to an even higher level of importance. The identification, evaluation, qualification, and selection of suppliers is challenging for domestic sourcing. Doing it globally is much more difficult, time-consuming, and costly.

Supply management's responsibilities for sourcing outside the United States are really no different than they are for finding domestic suppliers; however, there are additional considerations that must be addressed in areas such as category management, *supplier relationship management* (SRM), and *total cost of ownership* (TCO). The concept of TCO is defined as the "sum of all costs associated with acquisition, use, ownership, and disposal of any organizational purchase." The application of this technique is particularly valuable when a firm is making offshore sourcing and buying decisions.

The primary reason for the shift from domestic to foreign sourcing has been cost reduction. This is why an up-front TCO analysis is important—to validate or invalidate the assumption of cost savings. Offshore buying does not always result in the expected cost savings. The geographic location, infrastructure, characteristics of the labor force, culture, and political or legal environment will all influence the comparative costs of sourcing around the world. Each must be factored into a TCO analysis.

The elements of TCO provide a quick analysis and decision-making structure, as seen in Table 4-1.

Supplier Relationship Management

One of the major changes in the way suppliers are managed is a move away from an arm's-length, adversarial relationship between buying and selling firms to a more collaborative perspective. SRM efforts reflect that change. SRM is not a software package. Software is a tool that facilitates but does not substitute for a well-structured and practiced method of managing supplier relationships. SRM includes guidance in how that relationship is to be managed and the processes by which this is accomplished. There are no universal ways to manage suppliers, and every situation will be different. What SRM does is set up a means of establishing mutual expectations, facilitating regular communication, and resolving issues.

How a firm views suppliers makes a big difference in the way supplier relationships are handled. A strategic focus is long-term oriented and cost driven; a tactical focus is short-term oriented and price driven. Table 4-2 illustrates how

TABLE 4-1 Examples of Major TCO Components

Acquisition Costs	
Price	**Landed Costs**
Supplier identification, evaluation, selection	✓ Taxes, tariffs, and duties
Sourcing administration	✓ Duties
Transportation	✓ Shipping
Regulatory compliance	✓ Insurance
	✓ Delivery
	✓ Documentation

Use Costs		**Ownership Costs**	**Disposal Costs**
• Setup	• Installation	• Taxes	• Environmental cleanup
• Tooling	• Training	• Insurance	• Salvage
• Conversion	• Maintenance	• Depreciation	• Contract termination
• Inventory	• Warehousing	• Shrinkage	
• Rework	• Handling	• Obsolescence	
• Scrap	• Service performance	• Cost of money	
• Warranty	• Supplier noncompliance	• Opportunity costs	

the philosophy regarding supplier relationships affects four important attributes concerning supplier management.

There are many types of supplier relationships, as seen in Chapter 3. Different types of relationships require different SRM methods. The greatest benefits come from the strategic alliances set up with key or critical suppliers. These benefits include improved value to the supply chain through collaboration in the following ways:

- Cost management
- Product development
- Inventory management
- Transportation management
- Product and process innovation

The interdependencies and the supply chain linkages between buying firms and their supply chain network require a well-structured SRM process. SRM includes the methods and the tools that companies use to develop and maintain

TABLE 4-2 Perspectives on Supplier Management

Attribute	Tactical Focus	Strategic Focus
Cost	**Price Driven** • Low bidder gets the order • TCO is not a decision factor	**Total Cost Driven** • TCO is used for negotiations • Target costs drive prices • Cost are jointly managed
Supplier Selection	**No Formal Process** • "Back door selling" • Little control of supplier selection	**Systematic Process** • Strategic sourcing drives decisions
Supplier Relationships	**Transactional** • No trust or collaboration • Hard bargaining in negotiations • Focus on short-term pricing	**Driven by Strategy** • Critical purchases are made with key suppliers • Cooperation and collaboration are fostered • Information sharing occurs • Mutual commitment to quality exists
Number of Suppliers	**Undetermined** • No sourcing strategy • No supplier management strategy	**Strategic Sourcing** • Sourcing process is controlled • Suppliers' performance is monitored • Strategy determines the number and type of suppliers

collaborative working relationships with suppliers. For example, the *key performance indicators* (KPIs) are measurements used to monitor supplier performance in critical areas such as on-time delivery, quality standards, and cost management. On-time delivery would be a KPI calculated as the percentage of a supplier's deliveries over a specified period that had been made on the date required.

SRM software is the tool that aids in the assembly, analysis, and display of the data associated with these KPIs. Interpersonal communications are also a part of SRM. Members of senior-level management as well as buying personnel regularly interface with key suppliers' management. These are top-tier suppliers who are responsible for critical parts or materials and support of joint-product development activities. Senior buying personnel, such as category managers, purchasing managers, or senior buyers, are the primary contacts within the buying company. They are the individuals responsible for the execution of the SRM processes.

Executives in such companies as major auto manufacturers place SRM high on their priority list. Mutual long-term value, not short-term price concessions, is their objective. Close internal collaboration may be required in order to achieve this objective and resolve conflicting departmental perspectives about what is important. For example, the quality assurance personnel might want to focus only on those suppliers with the best track records of conformance to quality standards. Engineering may want only suppliers with the highest technical capabilities and innovative ideas. Supply management personnel are the ones who bring together the various perspectives and create a unified approach to supplier performance assessment.

Still Struggling

Among automotive suppliers, Honda is recognized as having one of the top supplier management systems. This requires a big commitment of both financial and personnel resources.

The author's conversations with Honda personnel support published reports that Honda sources up to 80% of its parts requirements from suppliers. Therefore, supplier performance is crucial to the company's continued success.

Listed below are some of the resources Honda commits to supplier development:

- Full-time personnel are engaged in helping suppliers develop employee involvement programs.
- Full-time engineers in the purchasing department work to improve supplier productivity and quality.
- Technical support is provided in areas such as plastic technology, welding, stamping, and aluminum die casting.
- Special teams help suppliers resolve problems as needed.
- Honda's Quality Up program works directly with executive managers at those suppliers with quality problems.
- Honda personnel regularly visit supplier facilities.
- An executive exchange program exists between the companies' executives.

Automotive companies, such as Honda and Toyota, have spent decades developing their supplier relationship processes. Their methods will not work for every company, nor are they needed for all types of buys. Keep in mind that although they foster close collaborative relationships, their SRM methods are also meant to avoid complacency. Both companies and their suppliers pay attention to performance metrics and act on them. Without constant monitoring, the interdependencies of close buyer-supplier relationships can present risks.

Negotiation and Contracting

Negotiation

Real-life business negotiations are not what you see on reality TV or what people do at a flea market. Hard bargaining for one-time advantage in a single purchase at a flea market may be useful, but it doesn't foster a collaborative relationship. Supply management's responsibility is to negotiate excellent agreements that help provide a competitive advantage for the buying firm and are mutually beneficial for the contracting companies.

Supply management professionals recognize the value of a buyer-supplier relationship and use negotiation as a way to establish and/or enhance that relationship. Skilled supply managers focus on three core areas during a negotiation:

1. Preparation
2. People
3. Process

Preparation

Nothing is more important than preparation. "If you fail to plan, you will plan to fail" is a quote attributed to many people—and it's true. Much more time must be allocated to preparation than to the actual face-to-face negotiation session. Supply managers collect and evaluate a wide array of both internal and external information when preparing for a negotiation.

The characteristics of the supply market, the industry, and the individual supplier are all factors that impact negotiations. For example, in a market where the buyer is a relatively small player, suppliers are not always going to be motivated to reach an agreement. If the value of the amount of business offered isn't worth the supplier's effort, the buyer will have no financial leverage in the negotiation.

People

Companies don't really negotiate; countries don't really negotiate. *People* negotiate. Negotiators who understand the importance of interpersonal skills are much more likely to reach sound agreements. Such skills aid in establishing trust between the negotiating parties. Building trust is a major contributor to the creation of a good relationship between buyers and suppliers. Each party needs to disclose information, and the level of trust between them will help open up communication. Trust includes the confidence that neither party is going to try to take advantage of the other when sensitive information such as cost data is shared.

Agreements between buyers and sellers should foster cooperation and collaboration in the supply chain. The better the working relationship between them, the easier it is to do that. The best agreements are created when both of the parties accept that each has interests that must be met. The negotiation then becomes more of a problem-solving mechanism than a tug-of-war to see who the tougher negotiator is.

Process

Negotiations are not one-time events. Professional supply chain negotiations follow a pattern of activity in the process from start to finish. A buyer begins with initial data gathering. The following information is the minimum a good negotiator should have after a consultation with the stakeholders:

- A description of the item or service
- Knowledge of the intended users and sites
- Projected term of the requirement (such as number of months, years)
- Estimates of current and future quantities needed
- The date a contract is wanted

Information provided by the stakeholders establishes the type of specifications that will best satisfy the requirements. This detailed identification of the part, product, or service's characteristics will help answer some of these important questions:

- *The supply market for this purchase*—Does the supply market have many suppliers available, relatively few of them, or just one?

- *The type of supplier solicitations needed*—Is a *request for information* (RFI), a *request for proposal* (RFP), or a *request for quotation* (RFQ) needed?

- *Cost analysis*—Is a price, or a cost, or a TCO analysis needed? If so, which is best in this situation?

The negotiation process may begin by seeking competitive proposals from suppliers or making a decision to negotiate with just one supplier. Some of the most important characteristics that determine the elements of this decision-making process are outlined in Table 4-3. As the table indicates, negotiations for purchases with unique and/or complex specifications should have different negotiation process elements from those for more commodity-like buys. The characteristics of the purchase to be made dictate the type of solicitation methods used, the extent of buyer/supplier collaboration in determining specifications, and whether the pricing will be based upon competitive market forces or a cost target to be achieved through negotiation with the supplier.

If the negotiation process begins with obtaining competitive proposals from suppliers, a set of activities similar to the ones in Figure 4-4 is followed. As indicated by the flowchart in the figure, these activities begin with a request for information (RFI) from a supplier or a number of suppliers. The information received is then analyzed and used to help determine the contents of a request for proposal (RFP) and to choose which of the suppliers who responded to the

TABLE 4-3 Characteristics for Competitive Bidding or Negotiated Purchase	
Characteristics of the Requirement	**Negotiation Process**
1. Unique material, part, or service 2. Complex design 3. Early stages of the life cycle 4. Few suppliers	• Solicitation methods: R.F.I., R.F.P. • Specifications: Combined technical and performance applied in collaboration with supplier • Pricing focus: Cost analysis and TCO evaluation
1. Non–differentiated commodity item 2. Simple design 3. Mature stage of the life cycle 4. Many suppliers	• Solicitation: R.F.Q. two–step process to address required value–added services • Specifications: Industry standard (off-the–shelf) • Pricing focus: Market-driven , competitive bid

FIGURE 4-4 · A supplier solicitation process.

RFI will be sent the RFP. The returned RFPs are analyzed, and one or more suppliers are chosen for the negotiation phase of the contracting process.

The Rules for Negotiations

Another process-related activity includes setting ground rules that will guide the negotiation:

- *Participants*—Who they will be internally and externally
- *Negotiating principles*—The style of negotiation to be used
- *Agenda*—What issues will be important to the discussions
- *Logistics and location for the conference*—The buyer's site, the supplier's site, or a neutral location

After a supplier or suppliers have been selected from among the best proposals and the ground rules have been established, the formal negotiation process begins. This formal process is a means by which the parties will attempt to reach a mutually beneficial agreement. How long the process takes and how much effort is required varies by how much value is at stake. Complex, costly, long-term agreements can take months. Simple changes in contracted quantities or minor price adjustments could be done in a day.

A key part of any negotiation process is the actual face-to-face negotiating conference. Some negotiations are done remotely by telephone, on live Internet conferencing, or even through e-mail exchanges. However, supply management professionals consider it best to meet in person whenever there is significant complexity involved or when high value or high risk is at stake. This gives each party a better opportunity to thoroughly explore the issues on the table and look for mutually beneficial ways to meet those interests.

Rather than arguing over positions, negotiators look for ways to reach an outcome that benefits both parties. Achieving this end requires a focus on their genuine interests regarding the issues being negotiated:

- *Issues* are anything about which there may be at least the appearance of conflict between the parties. An issue could be something as seemingly simple as the color of uniforms worn by janitorial personnel to something as significant as how progress payments for a multimillion-dollar construction contract will be handled.

- *Interests* are the real needs of the buyer and the seller. These are not positions or the "one-right-way" of doing something. They are what each party must achieve to make the agreement worthwhile.

Still Struggling

How parts and products are packaged for shipment through the supply chain is very important. Packaging is a cost that must be managed while the safety and quality of what is being shipped is maintained. Therefore, packaging requirements can be a major negotiation issue for both buyers and suppliers:

1. The buyer's position could be: "You must conform to our packaging requirements without exception. That's not negotiable!"
2. The buyer's real interests are that all products arrive undamaged and in such a way as to be immediately placed in a work cell or production line.

The first example is really a demand. "Do it our way!" The second offers the buyer and supplier the opportunity to collaborate in finding the best ways to meet the underlying need for undamaged parts or products ready to be placed at the point of use.

This back and forth dialogue includes exploring various options and making concessions and trade-offs toward reaching agreement. It's important that the negotiators be aware of what alternatives to an agreement their counterpart may have. This often influences the potential value of various options and the willingness of either party to accept concessions or trade-offs.

- *Options* are the ways each party proposes that the two firms can collaborate in meeting their mutual interests. The more options that are presented, the more likely a good agreement can be reached.
- *Alternatives* are ways in which each party can meet their needs without the collaboration of the other. It's what they can do if no agreement can be reached. During the preparation phase of negotiation, the parties will each have looked for their BATNA. This is an acronym popularized by Roger Fisher at Harvard. It stands for *Best Alternative to (a) Negotiated Agreement*.

If you have ever interviewed for a job you didn't need, you've experienced the benefits of knowing your BATNA. What's the alternative of not getting that job? You just keep the one you have! Going into the interview you'd probably be calm and comfortable about the discussion. That's the power of having a BATNA— knowing what you can do if the negotiation doesn't meet your minimum needs i.e., bottom line.

It would be quite different if you had no alternatives; if this was the one and only job interview and you had no idea what you were going to do if you didn't get it. That's the power of *not* having a BATNA. It makes us nervous, less confident, and prone to making too many concessions.

Contracting

Under U.S. law, a contract is an agreement or a set of mutual promises, between two or more parties. The law requires fulfillment of those promises and provides remedies if the promises are not kept. Supply management negotiates and manages contracts on behalf of the organization. It is their responsibility to understand basic commercial contract law and those laws that apply to the international sale of goods. In the United States, Article 2 of the Uniform Commercial Code is the basis for contracts. Internationally, the United Nations Convention on *Contracts for the International Sale of Goods* (CISG) is the primary legal resource.

In legal terms, the contract really is more than the paper it is written on. That contract document provides hard evidence that a relationship has been established between the parties. Given the importance of the relationship, in the long term, neither party will benefit from a one-sided contract.

Contracts with suppliers are usually negotiated by supply management personnel in collaboration with internal stakeholders, including the legal department. It's essential that the legal professionals be brought into the process early to avoid any unexpected legal issues during or after the negotiation. There are often terms and conditions that will be required by the in-house legal group, and negotiators must understand them beforehand. Elements of the contract associated with the products, parts, or services to be provided must be flexible to allow supply managers an opportunity to create options and offer reciprocal concessions in negotiating the agreement.

Supply management's expertise in the contracting process is particularly important to service agreements where a *statement of work* (SOW) is required.

This is a negotiated document that clearly defines what is to be done, by whom, when, how, and the rights and responsibilities of the parties involved. The ultimate success of the agreement, the ease or difficulty of managing it, and the value of what is provided are critically dependent on how well the SOW is structured.

Cost Control

Creating and moving a product to customers is a costly affair. Logistics costs alone can amount to 50% of all supply chain costs. Therefore, no matter what supply chain strategy a firm uses, controlling supply chain costs is always a big headache for senior executives. Every transaction, purchase made, inventory stored, goods or material transported, product produced—every activity in the supply chain—impacts cost. The goal is to see to it that everything adds value.

As Figure 4-5 illustrates, savings are another reason why supply management is important—every penny they save by sourcing strategically can go right to profit.

- For a manufacturer, the cost of materials purchased to make the average product may account for anywhere from 25 to 70 percent of the product's *cost of goods sold* (COGS). For example, if it costs $100 to make a product, between $25 and $70 of that cost bought the direct materials that went into it.

- From a wholesaler's perspective, the biggest cost is for the goods and materials in their product line.

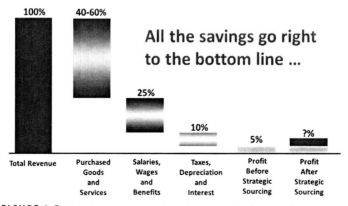

FIGURE 4-5 • Supply management's savings go to the bottom line.

The costs of purchased goods and materials represent the bulk of the dollars supply management spends, where periodic price increases often occur, and where negotiation may have a big payoff. Therefore, it's obvious why managing these costs is an especially critical responsibility for supply management professionals.

Improve the Value of Specifications

Everything a firm buys has specifications. Specifications detail the characteristics of a material, part, product, or service. They also show how something is to be made or how a service is to be provided.

There are many types of specifications, and each one (or a combination of them) can favorably or unfavorably impact cost. A simple list of four types of specifications includes the following:

1. *Detailed technical specifications*—Outline the design, materials, and method of manufacturing to be used in creating something.

2. *Commercial specifications*—Specifications that have been developed by industry associations. For example, the *American National Standards Institute* (ANSI) is one group involved in the development of technology standards in the United States. ANSI has thousands of specifications already established for a wide range of products and services. These specifications are known to and usually followed by suppliers, and therefore, items based upon them usually cost less to purchase than items that require conformance to a unique technical specification.

3. *Brand name*—A specification that calls out a very specific manufacturer (i.e., Kohler plumbing equipment, or a Dell computer).

4. *Performance specifications*—Identify what is to be done or what is to be accomplished rather than the details of how it is to be achieved. In the purchase of goods or materials, these specifications usually include form, fit, and function. In the purchase of services, performance specifications are often used to identify the outcomes the buyer wants the supplier to achieve. The supplier is then paid according to its ability to meet those outcomes.

The important thing to remember is that specifications drive costs. Supply management personnel can help control those costs. The first step in any purchase is the identification and description (specification) of the need. This is where the control of cost begins. The users who request a purchase of something may not be aware of the big picture—they don't always know what they don't know.

Buyers can help by suggesting more cost-effective alternatives, or locating something that could be purchased under an existing contract. They can work in collaboration with those who request a purchase and help evaluate the type of specifications to be used for it. Usually the more latitude buyers have in the type of specification, the more cost-effective their purchase can be. Buying personnel can also collaborate with suppliers to see where costs can be better controlled by amending specifications or the tolerances required, substituting parts or materials used, and eliminating anything that will not contribute value to the purchase.

Ways to Manage the Cost of Specifications

Here are key cost containment ideas that a buyer keeps in mind regarding specifications:

- Remember the final customer! Always keep the consumer in mind, and judge everything based upon what his or her perception of value will be.
- Avoid unique specifications. Use off-the-shelf products whenever possible because custom goods always cost more.
- Use commercial standards whenever possible. They are less costly because they are already known and used by suppliers. This also increases the number of potential sources.
- Focus on function. Be sure that the cost of anything matches the value of the function it provides.
- Use detailed technical specifications (material and method-of-manufacture specifications) only when the buying firm is the expert at developing them. Otherwise, use the supplier's expertise.
- Use performance specifications whenever possible. They make better use of a supplier's expertise and improve a supplier's responsibility for whatever the final product does or for the service it provides.
- Combine various methods of requirement specifications to improve overall value and quality.
- When writing the specifications, work as a team and address as many of the following considerations as possible:
  - Design and marketing requirements
  - Functional characteristics
  - Manufacturing issues
  - Quality assurance (robust design)

  ○ Material handling and storage requirements

  ○ Scheduling needs and procedures

  ○ OSHA and other safety regulations

  ○ All TCO factors

The following are some of the most widely used methods by which supply management personnel eliminate, avoid, or reduce supply chain costs:

- Create and deploy a strategic sourcing strategy. This will help to reduce unnecessary costs spent on purchasing low-value requirements and re-focus attention on the critical buys where there is greater cost-saving opportunity.

- Collaborate with suppliers on process improvements. Look for ways to eliminate redundancy in tasks or processes. An example would be implementing Internet-based transactions for orders and payments in place of paper-driven processes.

- Measure, monitor, and act upon the supply chain performance of all suppliers. Supplier nonperformance is a cost that proper SRM methods can reduce.

- Colocate supplier management personnel in the engineering and NPD groups where they can be in direct touch with the needs of these groups and minimize the time and cost required to fulfill those needs.

- Collaborate with suppliers and internal functions to map the supply chain and identify opportunities for waste elimination and reduction of supply chain cycle times.

- Analyze the reasons for inventory throughout the supply chain and implement actions to reduce it.

Innovation and New Product Development

In the development of any new product or service, a trade-off exists between cost and value. From a value-analysis perspective, anything that does not contribute value in the eyes of the final customer is waste. The vast majority of this cost or value equation is established up front in design and development. After that point, it's much more difficult to eliminate unnecessary costs.

Professional supply managers can contribute greatly to the success of a new product or service development. Time to market, product differentiation, cost control, quality assurance, and supply chain efficiencies are all areas where supply management's expertise and abilities are beneficial to the NPD process. These capabilities are not always used. The reasons why are varied. Sometimes it's simply a matter of unavailable resources within the supply management group.

The notion of integrating supply management personnel into the NPD process is a great idea that has been around for decades. Unfortunately this is still not a universal practice. These professionals can play key roles in helping to speed the NPD process, eliminate non-value-adding costs, and assure success of ongoing production once the products are released. Here are some of the major ways in which this group can help:

- Helping to assess any trade-offs in the cost and efficiencies of particular innovations
- Collaborating in the internal information exchange and decision-making processes required
- Sourcing suppliers for prototypes and then coordinating the transfer of required materials and parts to ongoing production suppliers
- Using a TCO perspective to gain an understanding of the best ways to minimize overall supply chain costs
- Coordinating with multiple suppliers where more than one supplier's capabilities are needed
- Negotiating contracts with suppliers who support either NPD or final production (or both)

Sometimes product development teams do not see what their supply management counterparts bring to the table. Many firms have overcome this obstacle by properly recruiting supply management personnel who have education and experience in both technical and business subjects. It's also a common misperception that buyers are always price driven. Whenever that is true, it is generally because the metrics by which they are evaluated have a misguided focus on price and not on total cost.

A "cheap parts fast" mindset can possibly be avoided by reviewing the personnel performance metrics and how they are weighted and then by rebalancing that scorecard. A professional buyer's analysis must rely on a total cost evaluation from a supply chain perspective. It may take a command decision from above to initiate the conversation between developers and buyers. However, once mutual understanding and respect are established, the benefits become evident.

Summary

This chapter has provided a brief glimpse into how the supply management function contributes to overall excellence in supply chain operations. Four indispensable ways that supply management supports supply chain network performance and enhances its value to customers are listed here:

1. Supplier management
2. Negotiation and contracting
3. Cost control
4. Innovation and *new product development* (NPD)

The development of complex global supplier networks has brought new recognition and greater responsibilities to supply management personnel, who are at the heart of *supplier relationship management* (SRM) and contract negotiations. They are the ones who help bridge the gaps between internal and external supply chain members. They facilitate communication and collaboration, which, along with the exercise of their professional expertise, gives them a primary role in managing costs across the supply chain and supporting NPD activity.

In the beginning of the book it was noted that supply chain management is all about managing the chain of supply. No functional area contributes more to that effort than supply management. In the next chapter, we'll move on to manufacturing and production, the "Make" element of the SCOR model.

Wake Technical Community College

QUIZ

1. The _____ step in supplier management is selecting the right suppliers.
   A. first
   B. second
   C. last
   D. easy

2. Out-tasking is done for something relatively _____
   A. important.
   B. costly.
   C. minor.
   D. strategic.

3. Firms _____ control the supplier selection process.
   A. cannot
   B. must
   C. should
   D. never

4. _____ refers to the process by which a firm identifies and selects suppliers.
   A. Buying
   B. Requisitioning
   C. Ordering
   D. Sourcing

5. _____ drive costs.
   A. Engineers
   B. Products
   C. Specifications
   D. Software programs

6. A contract is a mutual _____
   A. partnership.
   B. agreement.
   C. sale.
   D. gain.

7. When writing the specifications, it's best to work as _____
   A. a supervisor.
   B. a manager.
   C. an individual.
   D. a team.

8. Anything that does not contribute value in the eyes of the customer is _____
   A. profit.
   B. waste.
   C. necessary.
   D. helpful.

9. It's a common misperception that buyers are always _____
   A. overpaid.
   B. "price driven".
   C. easy negotiators.
   D. certified.

10. A _____ source is the only one capable of providing a product or service.
    A. sole
    B. single
    C. good
    D. local

11. _____ have been developed by industry associations.
    A. Commercial specifications
    B. Technical specifications
    C. Functional specifications
    D. Difficult specifications

12. In the United States, Article 2 of the _____ is the basis for contracts.
    A. Seller's Code
    B. State Sales Code
    C. Uniform Buyer's Act
    D. Uniform Commercial Code (UCC)

13. The measurement of a supplier's on-time delivery performance is a _____
    A. waste of time.
    B. KPI.
    C. financial indicator.
    D. product safety issue.

14. Supply management's role has gotten more _____
    A. fun.
    B. complex and challenging.
    C. humorous.
    D. complacent.

15. _____ specifications call out a specific manufacturer.
    A. Commercial
    B. Technical
    C. Performance
    D. Brand name

chapter **5**

Manufacturing and Production

If nothing is made for customers, it won't matter how well the other parts of the supply chain are working. Manufacturing is the transformational link in the supply chain that produces what both the intermediate and final customers want. To accomplish those ends, manufacturers need to create quality products that can be sold profitably to customers. Frequently, this goal is accomplished by using techniques such as *just in time* (JIT) and *Lean manufacturing* (Lean). Both of these methods require integrated supply chain management.

CHAPTER OBJECTIVES

In this chapter, you will learn

- Basic manufacturing methods.
- What manufacturers and producers do differently.
- The characteristics of five types of production operations.
- The principles of JIT, Lean manufacturing, and Six Sigma.
- How to incorporate manufacturing and supply chain thinking into product design.

This chapter will review the basic characteristics of manufacturers and producers, the types of production processes, and the widely used manufacturing methods. It will also illustrate ways in which a firm's internal and external manufacturing operations can be designed from an integrated supply chain perspective.

Understanding Basic Manufacturing Techniques

It is important for those in supply chain management to have a basic understanding of different types of manufacturing and production processes. That's because fewer firms are vertically integrated today. As previous chapters illustrated, it is much more common for a firm to have a network of outside manufacturers and producers who may create the majority of the components used in the firm's products. Knowing the suppliers' types of operations helps a firm to assess their capabilities, understand their cost drivers, and collaborate in maximizing the value of their contribution.

In addition, both external suppliers and internal personnel need to understand the nature of a firm's production methods. Today, more manufacturing processes are made to be flexible in order to respond to market changes and allow for the mass customization of products. This flexibility is often achieved by applying techniques such as JIT and Lean manufacturing, which require collaboration throughout the external supply chain network, as well as internally. For example, the personnel responsible for production planning and scheduling must decide how the available materials, equipment, and human resources will be used to manufacture products. Their work includes making decisions about the allocation of parts and materials for each product to be produced, the people required to do the job, and the sequence in which the production processes take place. Production scheduling can vary among firms, depending upon whether the operation is a flow shop or a job shop. The schedulers rely heavily on the sales department's forecasted demand in order to schedule production accurately. Supply management is responsible for acquiring the materials that production will need to meet that plan and managing the suppliers who provide them. The logistics personnel are responsible for the movement and storage of the materials. The point of this discussion is that the supply chain does not stop at the loading dock—it continues right through the transformation phase of manufacturing.

Manufacturers and Producers

There are two types of firms that make something: manufacturers and producers. In Chapter 2, the distinction between manufacturer and producer was briefly summarized as "Manufacturers are all producers, but not all producers are manufacturers." A little more detail on the differences will help clarify this idea further. Manufacturing transforms raw material and parts into a product by using a detailed set of specifications, a plan for what is to be done, and labor and equipment to accomplish it. Manufacturing includes processes that forge, weld, shape, extrude, and assemble. For example, an automobile company produces cars by manufacturing them.

Service providers also produce something. A writer creates a novel; a doctor produces a diagnosis. But neither of these two manufactures the outcome. They engage in intellectual labor in creating their output. The differences between manufacturers and service providers were illustrated in greater detail in Chapter 1.

In the agricultural industry, farmers are producers of food products. They grow crops and raise animals—but they don't manufacture them. Other types of producers include companies in the mining, petroleum, and forest products industries. Among other activities, producers plant, grow, harvest, raise, extract, and mine. In supply chain discussions, the term "producer" usually refers to organizations that are involved in supplying these types of basic foodstuffs or materials.

Producer's Supply Chains

While the focus of much of this book has been on manufacturing, it's important to recognize that producers have supply chains. For example, Figure 5-1 illustrates a simplified supply chain for corn. Farming is an excellent example of an integrated supply chain. It includes the factors that a farmer considers at the very beginning when designing a supply chain for the production process. To accommodate the characteristics of the supply chain, the farmer makes decisions regarding factors such as the following:

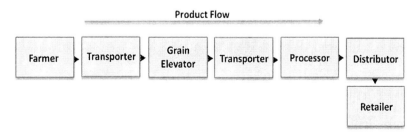

FIGURE 5-1 · Corn producer's supply chain.

- The type of corn to plant based upon the market into which it will be sold
- Field preparation and layout that will maximize land use and ease of harvesting
- The transporters that will be used and the types of storage the grain will encounter during transit through the supply chain

When the supply chain's design is considered at the beginning, the processes of planting, harvesting, transporting, storing, and processing can all be integrated and synchronized. Just as a producer links all these processes through attention to design, so must manufacturers.

Manufacturing and Production Methods

There are two types of manufacturing and production methods: *discrete* and *process*.

1. In discrete manufacturing, things are made through the fabrication of parts from raw materials or the assembly of premade parts and components, or by doing both. Assembly procedures are followed to create a product by using the items listed on a *bill of materials* (BOM), e.g., assembling electronic parts and other components into a computer.

2. Process operations turn raw materials into products through a series of mechanical, chemical, and/or biological steps. Unlike the outcome from

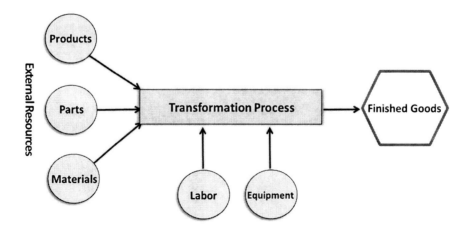

FIGURE 5-2 · Production process for computer assembly.

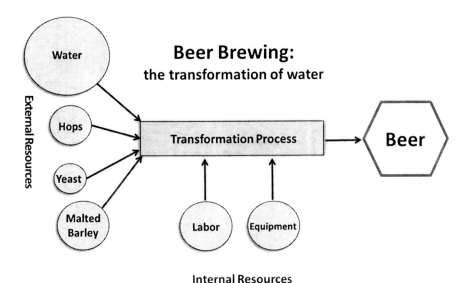

FIGURE 5-3 · Beer brewing process.

discrete manufacturing, the products produced in a process operation can't be disassembled. The beer example shown in Figure 5-3 is one way to illustrate this.

Process versus Discrete

Brewers use a recipe instead of a BOM to make beer. They put the ingredients in the recipe through a progressive series of controlled steps to produce beer. Once the beer is made, you can't take it apart and bring back the water, barley, hops, and yeast that created the beer. Through various operations and by the biological action of the yeast, these ingredients have all been transformed chemically into something completely different from their original makeup (the yeast actually converts the sugars of the mix into alcohol, which wasn't part of the recipe). But if you assemble a computer, you can also pretty much disassemble it into its original major components.

Types of Operations

There are five principle types of operations used to create goods or products: (1) project, (2) job shop, (3) batch flow, (4) line flow, and (5) continuous flow. The important ways in which these types vary include

- the variety of products they can produce,
- the volume of products they can produce,
- the flexibility they provide,
- the investment they require, and
- the amount of labor and level of skill they may require.

Figure 5-4 illustrates these variations for job shop, batch, line, and continuous flow operations. As the figure shows, the critical factors of flexibility and unit cost both decrease down the continuum from a job shop to a continuous flow operation. For instance, a small auto repair shop (job shop) has the flexibility to work on many different types of cars. An automobile or truck assembly line has a significant investment in high volume equipment that is fixed in place, which means it has no flexibility to create anything other than that for which the machines are designed.

All five principal types of operations exist in supply chains. Below is a brief description of each one:

1. *Project*—This method is used to create specialized or unique products or services. It could be used to construct a building, create an advertising

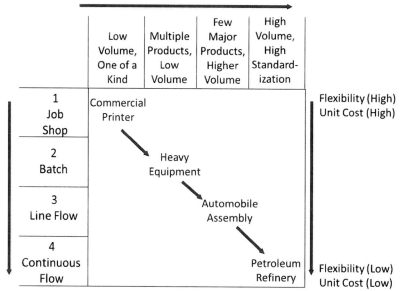

Adapted from: *Operations Management for Competitive Advantage*, 2006, Richard B. Chase, F. Robert Jacobs, Nicholas J. Aquilano, 11th edition, McGraw-Hill Higher Education

FIGURE 5-4 • Variations in attributes by type of operation.

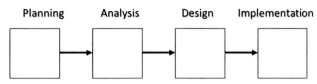

FIGURE 5-5 • Project flow.

campaign, or produce any special type of outcome. No two projects are exactly the same. Similar project management activities can be universally applied to them, but each project has a distinct and flexible process or set of processes. (See Figure 5-5.)

2. *Job shop*—Many suppliers are job shop operations. These companies often have several different customers for whom they make numerous different parts or products. So, they are frequently used by second- and third-tier suppliers who need the flexibility to produce multiple, customized products. Each of those products are to be made only when ordered. Each product might also have variations in its manufacturing processes due to any particular customer's requirements. A print shop is a common job shop operation. In the automotive industry, injection molding suppliers and sheet metal fabricators may be job shop operations. (See Figure 5-6.)

3. *Batch flow*—Batch flow processes and job shop operations are similar. The difference is that the number and variety of products produced is fewer and the volumes produced are higher in a batch flow operation. For example, a copy center is doing a job shop operation when printing a single copy of an item. If the center is running a hundred of them, it's a batch

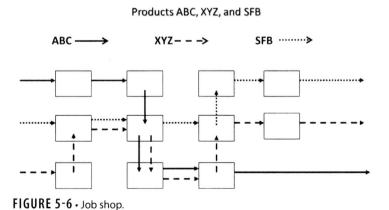

FIGURE 5-6 • Job shop.

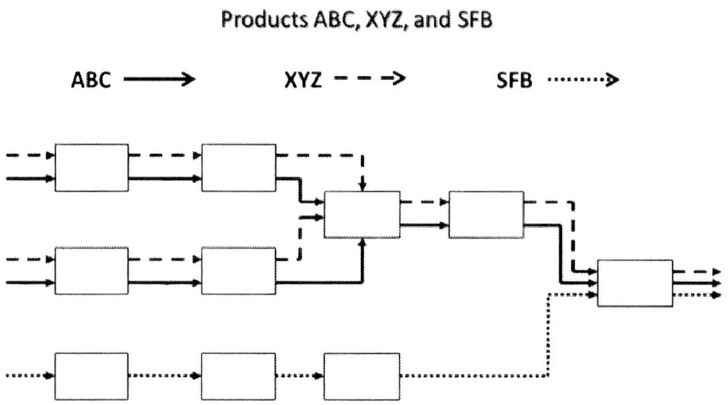

Products ABC, XYZ, and SFB

ABC ⟶   XYZ – – –>   SFB ·········>

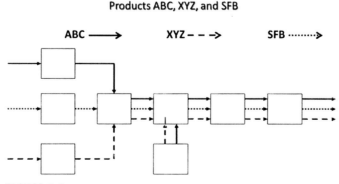

FIGURE 5-7 · Batch flow process.

flow process. Clothing suppliers, furniture makers, and bakeries are other examples of companies using a batch flow operation. (See Figure 5-7.)

4. *Line Flow*—Also known as discrete flow, the line flow process is sort of a hybrid between batch and continuous flow processes. It is used when there are a limited number of variations in the products but they are produced continuously in high volumes. For example, automobile assembly plants produce very similar products using very sophisticated, high volume machines. Cars are assembled in a sequence of linear processes where people and machines complete a series of individual tasks until the vehicle is complete. These same tasks are repeated again and again in a linear flow that produces high volume output over time. (See Figure 5-8.)

5. *Continuous Flow*—The brewer in the beer example would have a continuous flow operation. Continuous flow generally produces high volumes of

Products ABC, XYZ, and SFB

ABC ⟶   XYZ – – –>   SFB ·········>

FIGURE 5-8 · Line flow process.

Products ABC, XYZ, and SFB

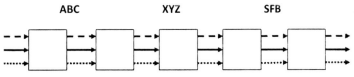

FIGURE 5-9 · Continuous flow process.

the same product. Food producers, steel producers, and petroleum refineries all use continuous flow operations. The raw materials that enter the process flow continuously through the system until the final product is created. (See Figure 5-9.)

Techniques for Process Improvement

Just in Time (JIT)

JIT is a technique used to eliminate the waste of excess inventory. Parts and materials are "pulled" through the production process only as needed, rather than "pushed" out onto the production floor in large quantities. Accountants justifiably see inventory as an asset because it represents an investment by the company. From a JIT perspective, however, it is an avoidable cost that must be minimized. Any costs that do not contribute to the value of the output are to be eliminated.

Although not called JIT at the time, Henry Ford used a comparable process of moving materials from the unloading dock directly to the manufacturing floor. The widespread adoption of the idea started when it was introduced by Taiichi Ohno at Japan's Toyota Motor Corporation in the 1950s. Toyota's production system evolved over many years as the philosophy of JIT became embedded in all of its processes. When creating new models, Toyota incorporated the concepts that could maximize its manufacturing efficiencies at the design stage. On the production floor, all processes were reviewed and modified. This led to modest improvements, such as the standardization of tools and tasks, and major innovations, such as the *single minute exchange of die* (SMED) process, which vastly reduced the time necessary to change tooling.

By necessity, the consequences of Toyota's methods moved from the factory out into the supply chain. For example, quality can be viewed as conformance to specifications. As Chapter 4 illustrated, specifications drive costs. If parts are not within specification, they can cause disruptions in the assembly process—and in their performance as part of the automobile. Toyota redesigned parts to make them more easily manufacturable and introduced *statistical quality control* (SQC) mechanisms to ensure the consistency of their quality. That attention to quality was also taken outside the firm to suppliers, since any defects in the parts provided by suppliers would also interrupt the process. Toyota worked with suppliers to improve their quality systems and delivery methods. The logistics system also had to be redesigned to guarantee that deliveries were made where and when needed. In a JIT manufacturing environment, late shipments can shut down the operation. Over time, companies across the world have adopted the Toyota production system.

Lean

Lean manufacturing or *Lean production* (Lean) is another method concerned with driving out waste. (See Figure 5-10.) In manufacturing, it is associated with a pull system, which means that customer orders determine the production schedule—they "pull" parts and materials through the manufacturing process. The objective is to maximize the efficiency of the manufacturing process through a reduction in downtime and raw material, *work-in-progress* (WIP), and finished goods inventories. To do that, the Lean process uses the set of tools illustrated in Figure 5-11. There are various opinions about the differences between JIT and Lean. A common perception is that they both incorporate the same philosophies, but Lean extends beyond production to the entire enterprise. This makes it applicable to services as well as manufacturing.

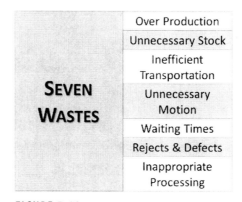

FIGURE 5-10 • Seven wastes.

FIGURE 5-11 • Lean tools.

To get the benefits of Lean, management must do at least these three things:

1. Accept that waste exists. A problem can't be solved unless there is awareness that one exists. The old adage, "if it ain't broke, don't fix it," is an impediment to getting people onboard with the Lean philosophy. Once processes are reviewed, the problems of inefficiencies and waste become apparent.

2. Find the root cause and solve it. Too often, only the consequence of a problem is seen and a Band-Aid approach is taken to fix it quickly. For example, as the section on metrics in Chapter 8 shows, the people are not the problem. It is the performance metrics that are driving the wrong behavior and causing the unwanted outcome.

3. Engage in continuous improvement. The *plan-do-check-act* (PDCA) cycle presented in Chapter 7 is also applicable here. Initiatives intended to solve a problem must be monitored to assess their effectiveness. Putting something in place and then walking away will not ensure that it works..

Six Sigma

Six Sigma is a method used to reduce variation in processes. Many of the same techniques that were developed for *Total Quality Management* (TQM) during the 1980s are among the tools used in the application of Six Sigma. However, a greater reliance on data and statistical tools in some ways makes Six Sigma an improvement over the original TQM philosophy.

All of these techniques have a place in supply chain thinking. The goals of each are compatible and their use is dependent upon the nature of a firm's business and supply chain design. Since the elimination of waste is an ongoing activity in supply chains, these are important concepts to apply continually. While widely known, there are still some obstacles to getting any of these methods implemented. Among those most often seen are the following:

- Lack of management commitment
- Failure to incorporate Lean thinking throughout the organization
- A focus on immediate returns versus long-term improvement
- A project approach to implementation instead of an embedded philosophy
- The inability to accept change

Design for Supply Chain Management

Just as the farmer's up-front supply chain planning results in better productivity, the collaboration among internal and external members of the manufacturing supply chain can do the same. The discussion of supply chain strategies in Chapter 3 includes a variety of ways in which companies could meet the demands of specific customer segments. Some of the objectives required to realize those strategies were dependent upon production considerations. In review, these three objectives were among those mentioned before:

1. Minimize the number of low volume products with unstable demand by reducing the complexity of the product mix.
2. Postpone the final configuration of products.
3. Create common product platforms and components.

These three goals are included in the four approaches commonly used to gain efficiencies in the supply chain operation: (1) commonality, (2) modularity, (3) universality, and (4) postponement.

Commonality

In Chapter 4, the use of common components, or standardization, was identified as one of the approaches that supply managers take to control costs. Too often, companies have developed and produced products that include a wide variation in components even in functionally similar products. However, if there is no performance, safety, or customer preference that mandates this, it's a wasteful practice. Whenever a part provides no value toward differentiating a final product, it should be designed to have the lowest cost specifications consistent with the function it serves.

The products could be standard, off-the-shelf ones made to conform to commercial specifications. They include things such as internal motors, electronic components, fasteners, power supplies, and transformers. The supply chain implications of using this approach are great:

- Reduced process costs from fewer part number to plan, order, receive, stock, and issue
- Reduced inventory carrying costs with fewer SKUs
- Reduced purchase prices because the higher volume of retained parts can be used to leverage the pricing
- Reduced life-cycle costs in warranty and product support

Modularity

The concept of using a modular approach to design and manufacturing is related to commonality. It, too, is about reducing volume—in this case, the number of individual subassemblies used to create a variety of products. Auto manufacturers do this extensively: they create a basic platform on which several models are made. The individual models are differentiated by the design of the exterior, the interior accessories, and the materials used, but the basic powertrain, braking systems, and suspension may all be the same.

There are some drawbacks to modularity. It cannot be used for attributes that are supposed to distinguish a product, including subsystems for washing machines, refrigerators, and automobiles. In the 1980s, Cadillac owners were dismayed when GM offered a Cimarron model that was much too similar to a Chevy Cavalier. Additionally, modules that are used across all product lines may be either insufficiently robust to accommodate the demands of top-end models or designed for the top end and too costly to use on low-end models. In either case, the benefits of sharing modules across models could be outweighed by other possible life-cycle costs and customer dissatisfaction.

Universality

In a 1995 article for the journal *Production Planning and Inventory Control*, Professor Hau Lee explained the way in which this method was used effectively at Hewlett-Packard in the design of a power supply. In the past, power supplies had been product-specific. He found that the long-term savings from using the same power supplies across different products was a substantial cost saver. Cost reductions were seen across the life cycle of the product from inventory reductions, lower repair costs, and transshipment costs.

Postponement

The term means what the word implies—to delay something because there are benefits in doing so. There are several ways to apply the idea of postponement. Most frequently it is associated with the final configuration of a product. The idea is to postpone the incorporation of the product characteristic that prepares it for the intended customer. This could be the final packaging and labeling required by retailers or, in the case of clothing producers such as Zara, even the color of the garment to be sold. These "last minute" changes are often done outside the producing firm by third parties in the supply chain.

JIT receipt of materials from suppliers is also a form of postponement. Automobile plants may have as little as four hours or less of inventory on the assembly floor. By leaving the inventory upstream in the chain of supply, the OEM avoids cost associated with handling, storage, and ownership.

An emerging process with potentially significant supply chain implications is *direct digital manufacturing* (DDM). The basic technologies of the process, three-dimensional printing and additive layer manufacturing, have been around for over two decades. However, rapid advances in the available materials from which products can be produced continue to expand DDM capabilities. This may bring new meaning to postponement. The possibilities include rapid production of small volume products customized to meet the end user's requirements.

Summary

The manufacturing or production element in a supply chain is the transformation stage where value is added in creating a product for customers. Therefore, it is important for both internal and external supply chain members to have an understanding of the operation's need for production. There are two types of production, discrete and process, and five types of operations. Each has benefits and limitations. In order to implement and continue techniques such as JIT and Lean, a firm needs to integrate their methods and techniques into the supply chain and appreciate how they can be employed. The best place to incorporate design for supply chain management is right up front when new products or processes are being developed.

The SCOR model of supply chain management processes—plan, source, make, deliver, and return—has been used as a basic template for the sequence in which this book's topics are covered. The preceding two chapters reviewed "plan" and "source," and this chapter covered the "make" element. The next chapter, on logistics, will complete this process by covering the remaining two elements in the SCOR model, "deliver" and "return."

QUIZ

1. Just in time (JIT) and Lean manufacturing require working _____ throughout the external supply chain network.
   A. overtime
   B. collaboratively
   C. on holidays
   D. nights

2. There are two types of firms that make something, _____ and producers.
   A. manufacturers
   B. retailers
   C. distributors
   D. wholesalers

3. Brewers use a recipe instead of a _____ to make beer.
   A. cookbook
   B. plan
   C. bill of materials (BOM)
   D. guess

4. The _____ method is used to create specialized or unique products or services.
   A. continuous flow
   B. project
   C. job shop
   D. batch flow

5. A _____ operation provides the flexibility to produce multiple customized products.
   A. continuous flow
   B. project
   C. job shop
   D. batch flow

6. _____ processes and job shop operations are similar. The difference is the number and variety of products produced.
   A. Continuous flow
   B. Project
   C. Job shop
   D. Batch flow

7. A _____ process is sort of a hybrid between a batch and a continuous flow process.
   A. parallel flow
   B. project
   C. job shop
   D. line flow

8. _____ generally produces high volumes of the same product.
   A. Continuous flow
   B. Project
   C. Job shop
   D. Line flow

9. Service providers and farmers are both _____
   A. subcontractors.
   B. great people.
   C. manufacturers.
   D. producers.

10. _____ is concerned with driving out waste.
   A. Process control
   B. Lean manufacturing
   C. A training video
   D. A labor contract

11. From _____ perspective, inventory is an avoidable cost that must be minimized.
   A. a vacation
   B. an outsourcing
   C. a government
   D. a JIT

12. Delaying the final configuration of products is known as _____
   A. placement.
   B. merriment.
   C. postponement.
   D. maintenance.

13. A method used to reduce variation in processes is _____
   A. Six Sigma.
   B. Six Flags.
   C. TCO.
   D. TQM.

14. _____ is a term for the use of common components, or standardization.
   A. Configuration
   B. Differentiation
   C. Commonality
   D. Proliferation

15. In the _____ process, it is necessary to find the root cause of a problem and solve it.
   A. Lean
   B. commonality
   C. payroll
   D. universality

chapter **6**

Logistics

Logistics plays a major role in successful supply chain management. Logistics personnel manage a host of activities, including what someone once called "the glue that holds the supply chain together"—transportation. The efficiency and effectiveness with which logistics functions are performed can be a source of profit or loss for supply chain members. This chapter will cover the primary responsibilities of a logistics department, review some of the critical decisions logistics managers must make, and illustrate the criteria they use to make them.

CHAPTER OBJECTIVES

In this chapter, you will learn

- Why logistics strategies are vital to organizational success.
- What the primary functions and activities of logistics are.
- What decisions logistics personnel must make.
- How many modes there are by which to ship goods or materials.
- What the trade-offs are in choosing transporters.
- What the responsibilities are of warehousing personnel.
- What *reverse logistics* means and why it is important.

The Basic Function of Logistics

As defined in Chapter 2, logistics moves and stores products and materials. This includes all inbound, outbound, internal, and external movements. Logistics manages the flow of inputs from suppliers, the movement of materials through different operations within the organization, and the flow of materials out to customers. It also handles the reverse flow, or reverse logistics, required for customer returns. The basic function of logistics is to manage the means by which an organization fills the gaps between members of the supply chain. A simple way to illustrate it is shown in Figure 6-1

Considerations for Logistics Strategy

Professor Donald J. Bowersox is credited with the logistics concept known as the *7-Rs*: assuring that the right customer gets the right product, in the right quantity and the right condition, at the right place, at the right time, and at the right cost. There is no single way for a firm to design its logistics network to meet those seven objectives. To accomplish those goals, a firm might rely on the oversight of a sometimes multifaceted system of distribution centers, warehouses, and stockrooms or something much more modest.

Creating a logistics structure that satisfies an average customer is not the answer. Neither is designing a strategy to meet the needs of the toughest customers. As shown in Chapter 3, not all customers' needs are the same, and a firm needs to implement strategies that cost-effectively meet the differences in customer segments. Designing a logistics network to do that can be a complex

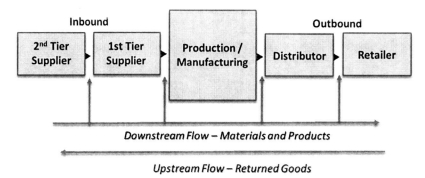

FIGURE 6-1 · Logistics fills the gaps.

decision-making process that includes choices such as how many warehouses to have and where to locate them, when to use third-party providers instead of company assets, and what inventories need to be held.

Retail Store Inventories

Some companies have taken an integrated supply chain perspective in order to find ideas for meeting the customers' needs. For example, bricks and mortar retailers have moved into the online space once held only by nontraditional retail firms, such as Amazon. There is usually little basic differentiation in the products they offer. Instead, the focus of their strategy needs to be service as a way to differentiate the customer's buying experience:

- Make it easy to locate and order online.
- Get the product to the customer quickly.
- Provide an easy way for customers to return products.
- Have fast customer service available for questions.

For traditional retailers, one part of that strategy is to utilize the inventory already held at store locations. Customers can shop online and then immediately pick up their merchandise locally. They can also avoid shipping costs by having items available only online sent to a retail outlet instead of their homes. The process for returning merchandise also involves the store. Customers can simply drop off the items to be returned and get credit on their account. Companies such as Home Depot and Sears have used this method for some time.

Cross docking is another practice used by retailers and distributors to reduce inventory costs. It involves the sorting of inbound shipments from different suppliers and consolidating them for immediate reshipping. Figure 6-2 illustrates the basics of this concept.

- In retail, cross docking entails taking incoming items and moving them directly into trucks for outbound delivery to stores.
- Distributors sort the incoming products from different suppliers and then combine them into shipments to fill individual customer orders. In both cases, the idea is to reduce handling and the cost of any intermediate storage for the inbound products.

Chapter 3 outlined a number of additional factors to be incorporated into a logistics strategy, including such issues as, the choice of transportation mode, use of third-party logistics providers, and inventory considerations. As this chapter

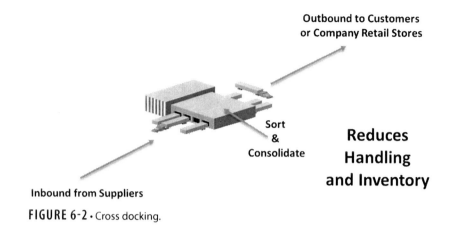

Outbound to Customers or Company Retail Stores

Sort & Consolidate

Reduces Handling and Inventory

Inbound from Suppliers

FIGURE 6-2 · Cross docking.

progresses, these will be addressed in the context of each of the logistics responsibilities that are outlined next.

Primary Logistics Activities

In Chapter 2, it was noted that the term *logistics* is currently associated more with a set of functions and activities that happen inside a company than anything else. In this chapter, we will review the six primary activities most often considered part of an organization's logistics function: (1) transportation, (2) warehousing, (3) inventory control, (4) packaging, (5) order fulfillment, and (6) returns processing.

Within these six activities are the three core functions of logistics: (1) transportation (inbound, outbound, and internal), (2) warehousing, and (3) distribution.

Transportation

This function's responsibility is to move materials and goods. If it were possible to move goods and materials directly from the point of extraction or manufacture to customers, transportation would be fairly simple. That is not the case in today's highly complex global supply chain networks. Transportation itself is a huge and complex business and is often the largest contributor to overall logistics costs.

Manufacturers have both inbound and outbound flows of materials and products. These flows vary considerably among types of manufacturers. For example, firms that produce automobiles or large appliances have many, many inbound shipments from suppliers—but fewer outbound shipments to wholesale or retail customers. On the other hand, a producer of food products or consumer goods may have hundreds of different individual products created from a much smaller number of bulk ingredients that arrive in rail car quantities. In this case, the number and type of outbound shipments is more complex.

A firm's transportation group is responsible for planning, scheduling, and controlling everything it takes to move goods and materials into and out of the organization. They need to prepare shipments for transit, decide on the size and the quantities in those shipments, and complete whatever freight documentation is necessary. Perhaps most importantly, the group must choose the mode or modes and the transport service providers used to move materials into and out of their company's facilities. *Mode* refers to the way in which something is transported. The service provider is the company that actually transports the goods or materials.

Choice of Modes

There are three general modes of transportation. Things can be moved over land, across water, or in the air. Each of these categories has various options available within them:

1. Land
   - Over roads utilizing trucks, tractor semitrailers, or tractor full trailers. (A semitrailer has wheels on the back and is supported by the tractor in the front. A full trailer has wheels at the front and back. A truck has no trailer.)
   - Over rails utilizing a locomotive attached to rail cars, such as boxcars, tank cars, or flat cars.
   - Through pipelines that transport gas or liquids through a conduit of interconnected pipes.
2. Water
   - Inland transportation across lakes, rivers, or canals, utilizing boats, barges, and ships
   - Ocean transportation using established sea routes for bulk or container ships
3. Air
   - Air transport includes primarily fixed wing transport aircraft flying into and out of commercial airports.
   - It may also include rotary aircraft such as helicopters.

Intermodal

The term *intermodal transportation* means exactly what it implies: it is a combination of the other transportation methods. For example, a container of goods may be transported to a port on a tractor semitrailer where it is then loaded onto a ship. Once the container ship arrives at its destination, the container is off-loaded to another tractor semitrailer, taken to a rail yard, and loaded onto a rail car. A train takes it to another location where it is off-loaded for final transport by tractor semitrailer.

The choice of mode is a trade-off among many factors: cost, timeliness, accessibility, reliability, safety, and security. In terms of cost, pipelines, water, and rail are the least expensive in that order. Using over-the-road transportation is more costly but much more flexible and faster than the other three options. Obviously, using airfreight is often the fastest for many types of shipments, but it is also the most costly. For instance, lightweight items such as electronic components or finished products are candidates for air shipment. However, large household appliances are most likely to be sent by rail, truck, or intermodal shipments.

There is no one right mode for shipping materials or products. All the factors associated with the trade-offs need to be analyzed before a decision is made. The final decision also depends on what is being shipped, including its size, weight, destination, required transit time, and perishability—all qualities that the firm's transportation group must consider.

Choice of Transport Providers

The choice of a transport provider is also not a simple decision. It, too, involves a complex set of variables that must be analyzed. The first step is to make a decision about whether or not to outsource transportation or do it with in-house resources. (This is a make-versus-buy or an outsourcing decision as discussed in Chapter 4.) Doing it in-house requires a private fleet, which has both advantages and disadvantages.

The advantage for some large companies is that a private fleet allows for greater flexibility in managing customer deliveries and direct control over costs and lead-times. That's why about half of all freight movement in the United States is done with private fleets. Besides the costs and complexity of managing such a fleet, another downside for many companies is the cost of the equipment and facilities required to do it.

For those who do not want or cannot afford a private fleet, there are many transportation service firms that are for hire. This, too, is a huge industry with lots of options available, including using common, regulated, contract, or exempt carriers. *Third-party logistics* (3PL) firms provide another option to be considered. These 3PLs offer a wide range of services that include more than just hauling the freight.

Once a decision is made to buy services, an individual company or companies must be chosen. Both the mode and the supplier are linked in this decision. The logistics group is going to balance three considerations in determining the mode and supplier: cost, time, and dependability.

1. From a total cost perspective, the fees paid to the service provider and the in-transit costs, such as insurance, need to be factored into the equation.
2. The lead time to fulfill orders is always a consideration but must be balanced against the costs of the fastest ways of doing it.
3. Dependability is a critical characteristic. Service providers who cannot assure performance to promised delivery dates every time are not suitable candidates for hire.

Options for Transportation Service Providers

There are many options from which logistics personnel can select a transportation provider, and they vary by the mode chosen. The brief outline below explains the characteristics of the choices available. (For this discussion, if it's freight, it moves on land by trains or trucks, and if it's cargo, it is loaded and moved on ships or aircraft.)

Roadway

Motor carriers transport materials and goods on roadways. A motor carrier can be an individual, an association, or a corporation. Any person or organization that either directly operates or manages one or more commercial motor vehicles for the purpose of transporting people or cargo is considered a motor carrier.

According to the American Trucking Associations' *American Trucking Trends 2012* report, in 2011 there were well over one million interstate motor carriers in the United States. The industry employed almost 7 million people and moved about $600 billion worth of freight. The companies in this industry are also predominately small enterprises, with 90 percent of the carriers having fewer than 20 trucks. How important is motor carrier transportation? The costs for all types of transportation combined contribute to about half of all supply chain costs, and most of that cost is for motor carrier transport. So, from a cost perspective alone, it is very important.

Rail

Rail transporters are generally grouped into four categories:

1. *Class I railroads*—These carry the bulk of the freight moved in the United States. They are carriers that operate in many states and generally move freight long distances.

2. *Regional railroads*—Defined by the *Association of American Railroads* (AAR) as "line-haul railroads with at least 350-route miles," these carriers usually operate in just a few states and have an operating range of about 400–600 miles.

3. *Local line-haul carriers*—These rail operations are usually confined to one state and provide short distance service.

4. *Switching and terminal (S&T) carriers*—These railroad carriers provide pick-up and delivery services for the line-haul railroads. They also move railroad cars between the different railroad companies.

Rail transportation is a major factor in the chain of supply. In the United States, the industry is dominated by seven very large Class I line-haul freight railroads. Statistics published by the Association of American Railroads show that in 2012 Class I railroads in the United States operated almost 139,000 miles of track and hauled over 1.8 trillion tons originated of freight (weight at its original point of shipment).

Pipeline

According to the U.S. *Department of Transportation* (DOT), "In 2003, there were over 2.3 million miles of pipelines in the United States carrying natural gas, and hazardous liquids (chiefly petroleum and refined petroleum products, as well as chemicals and hydrogen)." The DOT categorizes them this way:

1. Pipelines that collect products from sources, such as wells on land or off-shore, or from shipping, such as tankers for oil or liquefied natural gas (LNG), and move the product to storage or processing.

2. Transmission pipelines that transport large quantities of hazardous liquids such as natural gas or petroleum over long distance.

3. Distribution lines are a part of natural gas systems, and consist of main lines and smaller service lines that connect to businesses and homes throughout a municipality.

Water

Companies in the water or marine transportation industry primarily transport cargo on the oceans or on inland waterways. The U.S. *Bureau of Labor Statistics* (BLS) breaks them into two subgroups according to the type of equipment used: (1) deep sea, coastal, and the Great Lakes; (2) inland water transportation. Here's a list of the major types of equipment and their primary areas of use:

- A barge is a boat with a flat bottom used to carry heavy cargo such as iron ore and bulk commodities such as grain. Barges are most often used in canals, on rivers, and in larger freshwater lakes.

- Bulk carriers transport large quantities of commodities such as iron ore or grain stored within the vessel itself.

- Coastal trading ships have shallow hulls that allow them to travel near shores,

- Container ships transport goods in standardized containers that are part of an intermodal transport system. (The majority of finished goods shipped around the world are carried on container ships.)

- Multipurpose or general cargo ships have the capability to carry many different types of cargo in containers or in bulk.

- Refrigerated ships transport cargo that is perishable and requires a cold, temperature-controlled environment in transit.

- Roll-on/roll-off ships are generally large ocean vessels equipped with ramps that allow vehicles such as cars and trucks to be loaded (rolled on) and unloaded (rolled off) easily.

- Tankers transport liquids such as refined petroleum products, crude oil, and chemicals.

- Tugboats are small craft but they are important. Without these powerful little boats, large ships would not be able to navigate into ports. Their main purpose is to help larger vessels move around inside harbors. They can also tow crippled ships or push barges.

It's important to note that the individual members of the global supply chain network who provide marine transportation rely on an enormous public and private infrastructure. The global system is a truly vast network that includes the individual companies and their equipment that transport cargo along with the ports, facilities, navigational devices, and personnel that support the process. The extent and condition of that infrastructure can be a factor in choosing how and with whom to ship.

Air

There are many individual players in the air-cargo transport system, including: (1) shipper, (2) carrier, (3) integrator, (4) freight forwarder (or 3PL), (5) operations personnel (ground handlers), and (6) consignee. Each of these plays an important role in assuring that cargo shipped to customers arrives undamaged and on time.

1. *Shipper*—The shipper is the one for whom the transport services are being provided.

2. *Carrier*—The firms that provide airfreight transport services are known as air-cargo carriers. These firms use aircraft to move cargo from one airport to another. There are two basic categories of carriers:

   a. Cargo-only carriers' basic function is to transport cargo. These carriers use aircraft that have been specifically outfitted for that purpose. The interior of the aircraft is configured to allow cargo pallets to be quickly rolled on and off and to be secured during transit.

   b. Combination carriers use passenger aircraft to transport cargo in addition to their primary function of transporting people. These carriers store that cargo in the hold, or the "belly", of their planes. Industry estimates are that about half of all international air cargo moves on combination carriers. In the United States, only 10%-15% is transported this way.

3. *Integrators* are both carriers and forwarders, and they often have their own aircraft and trucking operations. Since airlines operate only between airports, integrators, such as FedEx, DHL, and UPS, are able to offer a full service operation to customers. They not only provide air transport for cargo but also the necessary trucking to take it from the airport to the consignee.

4. *Freight forwarders or third-party logistics providers (3PLSs)* act as agents for the shipper in arranging all the transportation required. When not using the services of an integrator, the shipper needs an agent to arrange for the other types of transport required to move the cargo from the airport to its destination.

5. *Operations management personnel* are needed to perform all the documentation, movement of cargo, and handling of aircraft on the ground. The International Air Transport Association estimated that by 2014 the international aviation industry would be handling 38 million tons of cargo annually. With such a massive volume of cargo to be handled globally each day, (over 100 thousand tons!), the management of it on the ground is a huge task.

6. *Consignee* is the one to whom the freight or cargo is being shipped.

Warehousing

This is another important function. Warehousing must receive, store, move, and ship materials or products. This includes internal movement and shipping to other locations such as distribution centers or customers. The people who manage the warehousing function are responsible for the following tasks: (1) the movement of materials or products, (2) storage of materials or products, and (3) managing information associated with those activities.

Movement

- The warehouse personnel must receive material or products from within the company and move it to a storage location.

- They must also receive and store goods or materials from outside the company. This will include unloading it from trucks, recording its receipt, and moving it to a storage location.

- They must assemble or *pick* those products that need to be grouped together to fulfill a customer order and get it ready for shipment.

- Warehousing personnel may also be responsible for *break bulk tasks*. These are needed when large quantities of a material or products must be broken down into smaller quantities for either storage or movement to other facilities

Storage

Products and materials may be stored for a short time or for a long term. In today's manufacturing environment, materials received that are going into the production cycle are usually stored for short periods before moving directly to their point of use in the manufacturing or assembly process. For most large scale manufacturing operations, a traditional warehouse full of parts waiting to be sent into production no longer exists. In U.S. auto plants, there may be no more than a few hours' worth of inventory inside the facility. If not replenished from suppliers in a just-in-time fashion, production would stop.

The consequence of the OEM's requirement for just-in-time delivery often means that the inventory gets shifted up the chain to the supplier. Sometimes suppliers must store finished or semifinished parts for a longer time so that they can avoid stockouts when customers order them.

Finished goods are stored until shipped to customers. This could be stock awaiting shipment from a producer to a wholesaler or from a wholesaler to a retailer's distribution center. Variations in stock holding patterns exist among the members of a supply chain. That variation and the topics of warehouse size, location, and stocking strategies will be explored later.

Information Management

Warehousing requires lots of information gathering, tracking, and reporting. Some of these tasks include the following:

- Receiving the materials and recording the information about that receipt
- Identifying materials and tracking their location as they are moved within the warehouse
- Monitoring the movement of any material out of the warehouse to customer or internal locations
- Monitoring and reporting stock levels

Inventory Control

This logistics function exists to manage inventories. The inventory control personnel help ensure that adequate levels of raw materials and finished goods are held in stock. Keeping track of how much inventory is on hand is a critical aspect of what they do. To be effective, inventory levels must be monitored continuously to be certain that the records of the amount and type of stock being held are always accurate. The need for replenishment of inventories is determined by how much is on hand and how much is required. Inaccuracy disrupts that planning process and leads to a surplus or shortages.

Inventory is a consequence; it is not an independent variable. Although the inventory control group is supposed to manage inventory, sometimes all they can really do is store it, count it, distribute it, and rotate it. The amount of inventory held is actually a result of many decisions made in collaboration with other organizational functions; it is not independently determined by inventory control personnel.

A manufacturing firm may have four principal types of inventory:

1. *Raw materials* are the parts, subassemblies, and other supplies that go into the products. In manufacturing, the quantity and type of raw materials inventory held is a balancing act between the right amount necessary to meet production requirements for parts and materials and the cost of carrying the inventory. Too much inventory on hand wastes money; too little available when needed can shut down production.

2. *Work-in-progress* (WIP) includes products that are not yet finished but are in some stage of the production process. The amount of WIP at any time depends on the volume of product being produced and the speed with which raw materials can be transformed into finished goods.

3. *Finished goods* are the complete products. Enough finished goods must be on hand to meet customer orders. Too much product in finished goods contributes the non-value-adding cost of holding it in inventory; too little creates the risk of not meeting customer needs and sales goals

4. *Maintenance, repair, and operating* (MRO) inventories are the parts and materials the firm needs to keep the facility and its machinery working. MRO stock can also be a source of wasted cost if not properly managed. Too much MRO stock risks adding the unnecessary cost of holding inventory; too little stock runs the risk of shutting down a manufacturing line or the facility itself because repairs cannot be made quickly.

In-Transit Inventory

Depending upon the transportation terms of the sale, a company may also include materials or products that are in transit as part of their inventory. Ownership of incoming materials from suppliers or outbound shipments to customers can be transferred at two points: the dock of the company that is shipping them or the dock of the company that purchased them.

If ownership was transferred at the selling company's site (F.O.B. origin), the buying firm owns them in transit, as illustrated in Figure 6-3. If ownership is

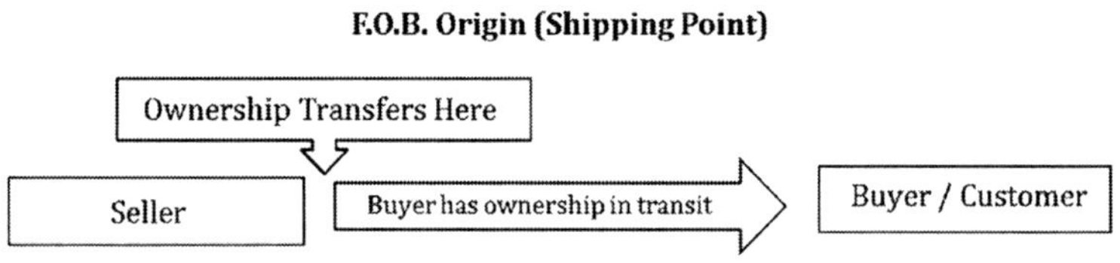

F.O.B. Origin (Shipping Point)

FIGURE 6-3 · Buyer is responsible for products in transit.

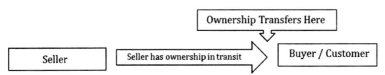

F.O.B. Destination

> Ownership Transfers Here

| Seller | Seller has ownership in transit | Buyer / Customer |

FIGURE 6-4 · Seller is responsible for products in transit.

transferred at the buyer (or customer's) site, the product or materials become the buyer's responsibility when they arrive, as shown in Figure 6-4.

All inventory management involves the constant monitoring of external and internal factors that may change the balance in the type and amount of materials held in stock. Whether it is on-site or in transit through the supply chain, inventory is an asset of the firm, and it must be managed from that point of view. Inventory control systems can use either a *periodic* or a *perpetual* method to do that. With periodic systems, companies choose to do either a regularly scheduled full physical count of everything in stock or do cycle counting. Cycle counting involves checking just a portion of the inventory on a regular basis.

The choice of inventory monitoring method varies among the different types and sizes of firms. For example in the retail industry, the cycle counting method is often used by smaller operations. But larger retailers rely on a perpetual inventory control system to track what's happening in real time. *Point-of-sale* (POS) information is captured at the checkout counter when bar codes are scanned. This system keeps the records of what is being sold and more accurately tracks on-hand stock, which is helpful for reordering merchandise only as it is sold. Such accuracy is important because either too much or too little inventory can cause problems. In a retail environment, lack of inventory (out of stock) can result in customer dissatisfaction and damaged revenue due to lost sales. Too much inventory results in spoilage, carrying costs, distressed sales, and ultimately lost revenue.

Packaging

There are two types of packaging: consumer packaging and industrial or transport packaging. Both enclose and protect products in shipment. However, consumer packaging is used for display and sale to final customers. The logistics function is concerned with what is called industrial or transport packaging. This packaging is often not seen by the final customer. It could be any type of container and other materials used to hold parts or products in transit to destination points along the chain of supply.

Order Fulfillment

Fulfillment of customer orders is a logistics process that has multiple sub-processes. An order must be received, processed, prepared, and delivered. Order fulfillment is vital in customer relations. The order lead time, that is the time between receipt of the order and delivery to the customer, is often critically important. Logistics must get the right product in the right quantity to the right place at the right time—and do so cost-effectively.

Reverse Logistics

Logistics personnel are responsible for processing products or materials returned by customers. This is known as *reverse logistics*. It includes all the processes required to receive returned products and determine what to do with them. When the costs associated with it become too high, reverse logistics can be a significant drain on profitability. When it's done well, it can be a great way to keep customers happy and coming back for more. Therefore, the primary objectives of this activity are to accomplish these tasks as efficiently and cost-effectively as possible.

Keeping customers happy while still meeting those two objectives requires good planning and a defined set of processes. The reverse logistics methods put in place must do the following:

- Include a clear process by which customers can return parts or products
- Identify, categorize, and count returned products
- Accommodate high variability in volumes received
- Include policies and procedures for recalls
- Determine what is eligible for restock, repair, or remanufacture and how this is to be done
- Manage the disposal of products that cannot be reclaimed
- Manage recycling and repackaging efforts

Once they get returns, the personnel in reverse logistics have several options from which to choose in deciding what to do with them. Among these options are the following:

1. *Restock for resale*—a returned product is acceptable to be resold as new.

2. *Recondition or refurbish*—a product is suitable to be just cleaned, repaired, and eventually resold as a new item.

3. *Remanufacture*—the product requires extensive repairs that may include completely disassembling it and replacing defective parts.

4. *Recycle*—some products are not suitable for any of the above actions but have parts or components whose value can be recaptured. This usually requires disassembling returned products and keeping some parts for reuse elsewhere.

For companies that excel at reverse logistics, such as Amazon, the results are satisfied customers and a competitive advantage in the marketplace.

Summary

Without logistics, there would be no way to get the materials needed to create products or move them to customers. The logistics function must balance several important activities that affect customer satisfaction and an organization's costs. Maintaining inventory levels that assure fulfillment of customer orders, selecting transportation modes and providers that guarantee on-time deliveries at reasonable cost, and creating distribution patterns and methods that get products where customers want them are some of the vital aspects of logistics management.

As with all other internal and external processes in the supply chain, excellence in logistics requires a dedicated effort to collaborate across functional lines inside and outside a firm. The benefits of a well-performing logistics operation enhance the competiveness of any organization.

QUIZ

1. Three core functions of logistics are: transportation, _____ , and distribution.
   A. production
   B. personnel management
   C. warehousing
   D. maintenance

2. A firm's transportation group is responsible for planning, scheduling, and controlling the _____ of goods and materials.
   A. design
   B. ordering
   C. marketing
   D. movement

3. Three general modes of transportation include movement over land, across _____ , or in the air.
   A. bridges
   B. borders
   C. water
   D. barriers

4. The term intermodal transportation means a combination of _____ methods.
   A. internal
   B. outsourcing
   C. transportation
   D. costly

5. The first step in making transportation decisions is whether to _____ it or do it with in-house resources.
   A. manage
   B. avoid
   C. accept
   D. outsource

6. _____ transport materials and goods on roadways.
   A. Trains
   B. Motor carriers
   C. Distributors
   D. Barges

7. The _____ is the one for whom the transport services are being provided.
   A. shipper
   B. consignee
   C. carrier
   D. producer

8. Freight forwarders or _____ act as agents for the shipper.
   A. truckers
   B. airlines
   C. transporters
   D. third-party logistics providers (3PLSs)

9. Warehousing must receive, _____, move, and ship materials or products.
   A. store
   B. make
   C. purchase
   D. design

10. _____ exists to manage inventories
    A. Purchasing
    B. Accounting
    C. Inventory control
    D. Production

11. _____ are the completed products the firm produces.
    A. Production materials
    B. Inventories
    C. Finished goods
    D. In-transit materials

12. _____ inventories are the parts and materials the firm needs to keep the facility and its machinery working.
    A. Raw
    B. Office
    C. Production
    D. Maintenance, repair, and operating (MRO)

13. Ownership of incoming materials from suppliers or outbound shipments to customers can be transferred at two points:_____
    A. retail or distribution.
    B. origin or destination.
    C. order entry or receipt.
    D. home or office.

14. **There are two types of packaging: _____ and industrial or transport packaging.**
    A. consumer packaging
    B. inexpensive plastics
    C. corrugated boxes
    D. foam enclosures

15. **Logistics personnel may choose to restock, refurbish, remanufacture, or_____ customer returns.**
    A. refuse
    B. take home
    C. send back
    D. recycle

chapter 7

Supply Chain Risks

Global supply chain networks have grown dramatically over the last two decades. Among the major drivers of such growth are the widespread use of offshore outsourcing, the opening of new markets, and the movement of production to low-cost countries. As a result of this trend, multitier and multichannel supply chains cross geographic and national boundaries worldwide. These supply chain networks are now large, complex systems with an enormous number of variables. Since all complex systems are by nature unstable, this situation creates numerous possibilities for disruption in supply chain operations. Failure of any link in the chain can be devastating. That's why effective supply chain risk management has become mandatory for the sustainability of any enterprise. Some of the main risks that exist for supply chain management and the methods by which firms are dealing with them are explored in this chapter. Also, events that led to major supply chain failures are provided as examples to highlight the critical need for vigilance and collaboration among all the members of global supply chain networks.

CHAPTER OBJECTIVES

In this chapter, you will learn

- Why supply chain risk management is important.
- What the differences between voluntary and involuntary risk are.

- How risks are defined, identified, and managed.
- What some of the major risks in a supply chain are.
- How a supply chain risk management system is developed.
- What caused some catastrophic supply chain failures and what could have prevented them.

Necessity for Risk Management

No firm can operate independently today. In the past, most of what a firm required to produce a finished product was made or provided internally. That's no longer true. For example, in the manufacturing sector, automotive companies purchase up to 80 percent or more of the components they need to create a vehicle. In the services sector, finance, insurance, and consulting firms have outsourced work to service providers around the globe.

The cost benefits of outsourcing manufacturing or services have been a key motivation for this trend. At the same time, organizations have also adopted strategies that made dependence on those outside providers ever more critical. Lean supply chain practices, supplier consolidation and rationalization, and inventory reduction are among the strategies used to build cost-effective supply chains; however, the smaller the cushion a firm has to absorb a shock, the more likely it will be felt.

Reliance on complex supply chain networks makes companies more vulnerable to numerous risks, including catastrophic business disruptions. Therefore, it's essential to have policies and procedures in place to defend against these vulnerabilities. Financial firms, such as banking and insurance, have long used classical risk management techniques, but only recently have those techniques been applied to supply chains. The type of risk management strategy employed is dependent on the nature of the risk exposure that must be managed. This in turn depends on the industry, the company, and the characteristics of the company's supply chain. Supply chain management professionals are still refining these strategies even as they are continually advancing the knowledge and skills necessary to manage supply chain risks.

Risk Defined

We encounter risk throughout the day without ever thinking about it. According to the National Safety Council, a pedestrian has about one chance in fifty thousand of being in a fatal accident each year. Waiting for a traffic light, using crosswalks, and looking both ways before stepping into the street are all methods we use to mitigate the risk of personally becoming that one in fifty thousand people who won't make it to the other side.

Some risks are unavoidable and some we choose:

- *Involuntary risks* are the consequences of events that happen without our consent, such as changes in weather. We have no choice regarding weather conditions and no control over the event itself. All we can do is try to minimize its negative effects. For example, we can't control a change in weather that produces a risk of rain, but we can mitigate its effects by carrying an umbrella.

- *Voluntary risks* are hazardous things we choose to do. We have a choice not to do those things. If we choose to do them, we can also choose to mitigate their possible negative outcomes. People who ride motorcycles or skydive accept that there are risks of injury from doing so. Motorcyclists wear helmets, and skydivers carefully pack their parachutes for the same reason—to mitigate the risk that what they choose to do will cause them injury.

Risk, *level of risk*, and *supply chain risk management* are three important concepts. Because the term "risk" has a variety of meanings, it's necessary to clarify how those three terms are defined in this chapter:

1. A risk in supply chain management is anything that could disrupt the ability of the supply chain to meet its goals.

2. Level of risk is a measure of the probability that an event will occur and the consequences of its occurrence. The probability of a severe earthquake where a key supplier is located may be small, but the consequences of one could be catastrophic. This would be a high-risk event.

3. Supply chain risk management is a method of identifying, analyzing, monitoring and preemptively controlling the consequences of events that could disrupt supply chain activity. It requires planned and organized collaboration among all supply chain members.

Supply Chain Risk Management Process

Successful supply chain management requires some risk taking. It is management's job to balance risks and rewards in decision making. The issue is really not whether risks should ever be taken; the issue is having an embedded mechanism to evaluate and manage both voluntary and involuntary risks, as necessary. There are many risk management methods that can help in making those decisions. They range from using simple checklists to employing complex software analytics that mine a database of internal and external data in order to search for trends and patterns.

Steps in a Supply Chain Risk Management Process

The process used to create and implement a supply chain risk management system follows a progression of tasks. Similar to a common format, the tasks are to identify, analyze, plan, track, and control. As illustrated in Figure 7-1, tasks and their labels are modified somewhat in order to reflect a supply chain risk perspective.

Scan the Internal and External Environment

The environment in which an organization exists has internal and external components. These must both be scanned to assess any factors that will have an impact on supply chain operations. This process is similar to a SWOT (strengths, weaknesses, opportunities, threats) analysis, which is a strategy covered in Chapter 3. In this application, the focus is more on identifying the weaknesses and threats as they relate to supply chain operations and management.

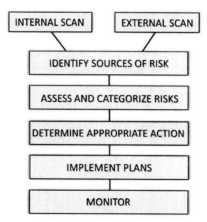

FIGURE 7-1 · A supply chain risk management process.

Internal Analysis

Analyzing the internal environment is the first step. It includes organizational structure, staffing levels, capabilities assessments, and the like. Supply chain management integrates essential business processes both inside and outside a company. Therefore, an organization's internal processes must be evaluated for their capability to support supply chain integration. Key processes would include those such as the following:

- Strategic planning at both the organizational and functional levels
- *Sales and operations planning* (S&OP)
- Production/operations
- *New product development* (NPD)
- Supplier relationship and customer relationship
- Business continuity and the supply chain risk management process

External Analysis

The external factors that could be investigated are endless. Each list will be unique to an individual organization as will the factors that are most likely to become sources of risk for that organization. The PESTEL analysis method, also discussed in Chapter 3, is one way to categorize the six major external factors:

1. *Political*—Politics at the local, national, and international level can have an impact on supply chain operations. For example, existing or proposed changes in laws, trade agreements, tariffs, and government-imposed trade sanctions need to be investigated.

2. *Economic*—Global supply chains require the assessment of local, regional, national, and international economies. Any trend or potential changes can influence sourcing opportunities and costs.

3. *Social*—Along with general demographic changes, changing public perceptions must be monitored. Shifting trends can reduce demand that would influence material requirements. Sustainability issues may also become more important, as increasing public awareness creates demands for more attention to *corporate social responsibility* (CSR) initiatives.

4. *Technological*—Modern supply chain management could not exist without the technological advances of the last few decades. New technologies improve communications, and *collaborative planning, forecasting, and*

replenishment (CPFR) support supply chain activity. However, regional or geographic weaknesses in technology infrastructure will negatively influence sourcing decisions and the potential for buyer-supplier collaboration.

5. *Environmental*—In this case, the natural environment is the concern. Supply chains are dependent on suppliers in areas subject to natural disasters. They also rely on transportation systems that are affected by weather.

6. *Legal*—Local, national, and international laws change. Patent protection, intellectual property rights, labor laws, and local content legislation are some of the key legal issues to be investigated.

In addition to categorizing the six factors in the PESTEL outline, the external scanning needs to include other elements, such as the characteristics of the sales markets for the company's products and services and the characteristics of the supply markets for required materials and services.

Identify Sources of Risk

Once all the information for an analysis of the organization's environment has been gathered and analyzed, the next step in the process is to look for sources of risk. As mentioned before, each supply chain risk assessment will be unique to the individual firm that does it. However, there are many sources of risks that are known to apply to any business, and some of these are described in the following sections.

Internal Sources of Risk

One positive aspect to internal sources of risk is that an organization has the ability to directly control them. Many risk factors may already be mitigated by existing policies and procedures. Those that are not must be addressed. Below are some common sources of internal risk:

- *Business continuity and supply chain risk management processes* are at the top of the list because a failure to have these processes in place would make any activity on the others irrelevant.

- *Communication and performance metrics* are the next two on this list because they influence internal collaboration. Anything that impedes communication and collaboration internally will result in costly inefficiency that will extend to the external supply chain. Internal performance metrics must be aligned with the requirements of organizational and supply chain goals rather than with individual functional departments. Measuring buyers on prices paid alone sets up a sure path to risky behavior. A change to a total cost perspective would encourage internal collaboration and better long-term results.

- *Employee skills* that are not consistent with those required for effective supply chain management can become sources of risk. Supply chain professionals need the knowledge and the skills to engage in cost analysis (particularly TCO) so that risky, wasteful decisions are not made. Employees must be available to rigorously select and manage suppliers to minimize the possibility of poor choices. Individuals who understand transportation modes, routes, and processes are assets in keeping the supply chain "glued" together and reacting quickly to impending transportation risks.

- *IT infrastructure* is a backbone of supply chains. Organizations need the internal capability to integrate communication, planning, forecasting, and financial processes into the supply chain network's system. Those that cannot are open to risk from many sources: poor communications, inadequate planning, forecast errors, and financial losses.

- *Staffing levels* can provide short-term savings and cause long-term disasters. Without adequate personnel to properly identify and manage sources of risk, there is little doubt that unintended consequences could prove costly.

External Sources of Risk

Mapping the supply chain network, its constituent members, and its structure should be the first activity in identifying interactions and common constraints that could be sources of risk. There is no one right answer to how extensively this should be done. For example, first-tier suppliers should always be included. However, the need to include interactions with second- and third-tier suppliers in the map will depend on the source of risk attributed to them. If a first-tier supplier could be catastrophically impacted by risk from an upstream supplier, that second- or third-tier supplier should be included.

Maps can help locate the root causes of risks by providing a visual perspective. They make complexity, redundancy, interconnections, and choke points more evident than is possible by reading a written report. Done with a global projection, they can also illustrate the distances and geographic implications that exist with international members of the supply chain network.

Even a simple map like the one in Figure 7-2 can be an aid in visualizing the potential risks in the supply chain. With the knowledge gained from the scan

Find Sources of Risk

- See the members from local or global perspectives
- Find interdependencies
- Look for weaknesses
- See complexity

FIGURE 7-2 · Simple supply chain map.

of the firm's environment, someone just looking at the map may see where problems might occur.

Some external sources of risk are identified below:

1. *Natural disasters* can present minor or major risks. Something as simple as a snowstorm could be a problem. In Chicago, it would take a blizzard to be disruptive, but in Atlanta, a few inches of snow could shut things down. Among other natural disasters are:

   • Earthquakes

   • Hurricanes

   • Floods

   • Drought

2. *Cultural differences* can affect negotiations, labor relations, production schedules, communications, and lead times. They include the following:

   • Ethical norms

   • Holidays

   • Religious observances

   • Languages

   • Styles of communication

   • Decision-making processes

3. *Security and privacy risks* are both domestic and international concerns. Loss of intellectual property, embezzlement, counterfeit parts, and destruction of property are some of the possible consequences. These risks can involve:

   - Fraud
   - *Intellectual property* (IP) theft
   - Terrorism
   - Data security
   - Proprietary data

4. *Financial risks* affect the bottom line and the firm's ability to do business. Inadequate working capital or limited access to financing can cripple a company or its suppliers. Especially for smaller suppliers, payment terms and cash flow can be critical to maintaining their operations. Sources of financial risk include:

   - Financing availability
   - Supplier liquidity
   - Accounts payables terms
   - Access to capital
   - Cash flow
   - Working capital availability
   - Inflation
   - Currency valuations

5. *Labor risks* to the firm are possible both internally and externally. Lack of skilled personnel can hamper production. Increasing wages and salaries drive up costs. Strikes or work stoppages affect production and sales. Labor risks include:

   - Lack of available labor
   - Rapidly escalating salaries
   - Unionizing activity
   - Labor market changes
   - Lack of skilled workers
   - Training requirements

6. *Control of a function* that is a strategic asset can be a problem when third parties are assigned that responsibility. This can result in a risk of delays, cost overruns, and loss of business. Those risks can arise in:

- Manufacturing
- Customer service
- *Information technology* (IT)
- Quality control
- Project management

7. *Supplier performance* is one of the most significant sources of risk in this category. Supplier nonperformance could produce consequences that range in impact from negligible to catastrophic. Failure to deliver what is required and when it is required can cause substantial costs for the buying firm. A failure to meet quality standards can result in production delays or field failures that have an impact on brand image and result in expensive recalls. Suppliers who are not financially sound may cease operations. Sources of such risks can be found in the following:

- Supplier performance
- Supplier finances
- Supplier capacity constraints
- Supplier capabilities

8. *Political issues* are sometimes difficult to assess. What is often called "stroke of pen" events can change the dynamics of a business overnight. Changes in regulatory requirements may eliminate current or potential sources of supply. Tighter compliance requirements can delay shipment for unanticipated inspection. Tariff rules can eliminate expected benefits of offshore sourcing. Political issues include:

- Regulatory requirements
- Changing tariffs
- Trade agreements
- New laws
- Political instability
- War or insurrection
- Import compliance
- Visas requirements

Assess and Categorize Risks

The next step in the risk assessment process is to analyze the sources of risk for their potential impact on the firm. Two factors determine the level of risk: the probability that an event will happen and the effect of that event's consequences. If enough historical information is available, some probabilities can be rather easily assessed. When hard data are not available or there is a high degree of uncertainty about the event or its resulting impact, some firms use complex mathematical algorithms to determine probabilities. In those cases, assessing the level of risks can be done using either quantitative or qualitative methods.

1. *Quantitative analysis* is a technique that uses complex mathematical and statistical modeling, such as simulations or decision-tree analysis. It is a way of measuring things with numbers.

2. *Qualitative analysis* is an iterative process used to evaluate available data and look for patterns or common themes. This method requires a rigorous and systematic approach to get meaningful results. Qualitative analysis is usually faster and less costly than quantitative methods and, unlike quantitative methods, does not use statistics.

One way to assign a relative value to the consequences is to look at the time and costs required to recover from the results of an event and how that will affect the firm financially. It can help to put the impacts of an event into logical categories depending on their severity. The chart in Figure 7-3 illustrates this

NEGLIGIBLE	MINOR	MODERATE	MAJOR	CATASTROPHIC
THIS IS A MINOR PROBLEM THAT CAN BE EASILY RESOLVED WITH LITTLE OR NO FINANCIAL IMPACT.	THIS WOULD CAUSE A MODEST DISRUPTION IN OPERATIONS AND HAVE A FINANCIAL IMPACT UP TO $X.	THIS WOULD HIGHLY DISRUPT OPERATIONS AND HAVE A FINANCIAL IMPACT UP TO $XX.	THIS WOULD SEVERELY DISRUPT OPERATIONS AND HAVE A FINANCIAL IMPACT UP TO $XXX.	THIS COULD CAUSE THE FIRM TO FAIL. DAMAGES COULD EXCEED THE FIRM'S ABILITY TO RECOVER.

FIGURE 7-3 • Categories of impact from an event.

PROBABILITY	CONSEQUENCES				
	NEGLIGIBLE	MINOR	MODERATE	MAJOR	CATASTROPHIC
ALMOST CERTAIN > 90%	1A	2A	3A	4A	5A
LIKELY BETWEEN 50-90%	1B	2B	3B	4B	5B
MODERATE BETWEEN 10-50%	1C	2C	3C	4C	5C
UNLIKELY BETWEEN 5 – 10%	1D	2D	3D	4D	5D
RARE < 5%	1E	2E	3E	4E	5E

FIGURE 7-4 · Risk assessment matrix.

concept. Once the categories of risk have been established and labeled, they can then be used to create a risk-assessment matrix, as illustrated in Figure 7-4.

In this example, potential consequences are labeled from negligible to catastrophic and numbered from 1 to 5 in the same order. The probability is labeled from rare to certain and labeled alphabetically. This method provides an easy way to identify the level of risk both graphically and in text. For example, a risk identified as a category 5A would be recognized as having catastrophic consequences and an almost certain likelihood of happening. Correspondingly, a risk labeled 1E is easily seen as nothing to worry about.

As seen in Figure 7-5, this is the step in which risk management alternatives need to be assessed for each major risk that is identified and the priorities established for the actions to be taken. The first priority is to determine the most acceptable methods for managing the extreme levels of risk. They are the ones that have the capacity to cause significant harm to the organization and need to be addressed immediately. Action on the remaining risks can be prioritized based on their impact, the ease of implementing corrective actions, and the available resources.

There are many alternative risk management strategies and methods in use. The five listed here are the most common practices from which supply chain personnel may choose:

1. *Eliminate*—To eliminate risk, a firm must remove the potential event that would cause a problem. During the financial crisis of 2007–2008, some companies were faced with the possibility that sole suppliers of key materials would fail and go out of business. In some cases, the buying com-

RISK ASSESSMENT MATRIX

PROBABILITY	CONSEQUENCES				
	NEGLIGIBLE	MINOR	MODERATE	MAJOR	CATASTROPHIC
ALMOST CERTAIN > 90%	1A	2A	3A	4A	5A
LIKELY BETWEEN 50-90%	1B	2B	3B	4B	5B
MODERATE BETWEEN 10-50%	1C	2C	3C	4C	5C
UNLIKELY BETWEEN 5 – 10%	1D	2D	3D	4D	5D
RARE < 5%	1E	2E	3E	4E	5E

RELATIVE LEVEL OF RISK

LOW	MODERATE	HIGH	EXTREME

FIGURE 7-5 • First priorities for action.

pany chose to purchase the supplier as a means of assuring the continuation of the supplier's operation.

2. *Accept*—Firms choose to accept risks that are of very low impact. This may require no action at all or some modest approach such as minor changes in production schedules.

3. *Avoid*—To avoid risks, firms usually need to make changes. These could be changes in strategy, operations, planning, or specifications. For instance, an apparent risk for material price increases could be avoided by purchasing all the materials for a product or project up front. Supplier quality-related problems could be resolved by changing specifications to make them more easily manufacturable. Planning changes could involve postponing a decision such as waiting until weather forecasts are more certain about a storm.

4. *Shift*—Shifting a risk means giving it to a third party. For example, a lack of proper equipment or trained personnel might pose numerous risks if a company makes a product internally. By outsourcing the manufacture of that product to a more capable supplier, the buying company has shifted any risks associated with making it. The supplier's capabilities allow it to better manage the risks.

5. *Mitigate*—In order to mitigate a risk, a firm must reduce the probability of an event or its consequences. Offshore sources of supply may create a number of risks. A firm can decide to source a critical part or material

locally or regionally to reduce the probability of events related to distance. A grocery store cannot reduce the probability of a major winter storm. But it can mitigate the consequence of stockouts by having larger inventories.

In this step, it's also necessary to identify the resources that will be needed for whatever risk management practice is chosen. Key members of the external supply chain should also be included in any discussion. Senior executives must be ready to commit the necessary financing, personnel, and infrastructure required.

Components of Supply Chain Risk Management

Regardless of the type of risks, there are some main components of supply chain risk management that all firms should have in place:

- Use a TCO approach to decision making throughout the supply chain. Decisions driven by price, short-term objectives, or "what everybody else is doing" are not good practice. This includes decisions regarding outsourcing, supplier selection, facility locations, parts and materials used in production, and offshore sourcing, or any other decision that could contribute to a performance failure in the supply chain.

- *Supplier Relationship Management* (SRM) is a critical component of risk management in global supply chain networks. To be effective, it must be a key element in the sourcing and supply management system. (Chapter 4 reviewed the SRM process in depth.) Supplier selection is particularly critical when the sources of supply are located in foreign countries. Neglecting due diligence in this process to save money up front merely opens the door to a myriad of downstream risks. Lack of communication and collaboration between buyers and suppliers can itself be a very big source of risk. That's because the formal and informal communication among supply chain members often reveals impending sources of risk that can then be acted upon more quickly.

- The supply chain's IT infrastructure is also critical. The extent to which information is easily shared among supply chain members is a major contributor to risk prevention. This is not solely the responsibility of one firm. Internally, companies must, of course, ensure that they have the technology, both software and infrastructure, to manage effectively. In the greater supply chain, the integration of shared or compatible technologies throughout the supply chain is a critical need. Transportation and routing management systems allow quick reaction to emerging risks. Product identification tools, such as RFID, allow tracking and tracing that is often legally required for some industries and could be beneficial to all. Standardizing payment, communication, joint planning, and monitoring systems should be a major goal for the principal members of a supply chain.

Implement and Monitor

These last two steps can and should be discussed together. Implementation of the plan should not be just internal to the organization. In fact, the entire development process should have included at least the major members of the supply chain. If the effect of the plan is to manage risk across the entire supply chain network, it must become an integral part of ongoing supply chain activity. Without both internal and external collaboration, this won't happen.

The process of managing risk is never ending. A proper reference for it is the *plan-do-check-act* (PDCA) cycle shown in Figure 7-6. This has been around for many years and is otherwise known as the Shewhart Cycle after its creator or the Deming Wheel of Quality after the man who did the most to popularize it. The first four steps in the process just outlined correspond to the plan element of the PDCA cycle. The implement phase is included in the "do" element of PDCA, and the monitor phase is the "check." But that's not where the process stops.

Monitoring includes gathering information, assessing its implications for risks, and reporting that information to management. Monitoring should be done continuously. Reporting can be at regular, but timely, intervals unless a

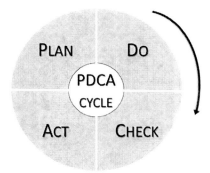

FIGURE 7-6 • PDCA cycle.

critical event is on the horizon. Any delays in reporting that make the information "old news" are unacceptable.

Beyond monitoring and reporting are the activities in the last element of the PDCA cycle: "Act." Obviously any emerging risks must be assessed and acted upon as required by their level of impact. In addition, actions taken previously to manage risk must be evaluated for their effectiveness and changed when needed. However, the risk management system itself must also be monitored. If it is found to be inadequate, the firm needs to act to remedy the situation. As shown in Table 7-1, there are many factors that should be evaluated because of their ability to assist or impede the success of a supply chain risk management system.

In summary, to be effective the supply chain risk management system must include these key characteristics:

- An organized, systematic approach across the supply chain that defines how, when, and what is to be done and who has the responsibility to do it.

TABLE 7-1 Two Dozen Factors That Will Influence the Success or Failure of Supply Chain Risk Management Systems

These help ...	These hinder ...
1. Clear and thorough requirements and definitions	1. Cross-cultural differences
2. Contingency planning	2. Inadequate contract development
3. A corrective action process	3. Inadequate management attention
4. Excellent governance mechanisms	4. Inadequate or poor communications
5. Excellent internal and external communications	5. Lack of a risk management system
6. Market knowledge	6. Lack of market knowledge
7. Performance metrics and monitoring	7. No contingency planning
8. A rigorous supplier selection process	8. Poor suppler relationship management
9. Senior executive sponsorship	9. Price-only orientation
10. Supplier relationship management	10. A short-term approach
11. TCO rather than price-driven decisions	11. Underestimated costs
12. An understanding of cultural issues	12. Weak negotiating skills

- Analytics processes that continuously capture information, analyze it, and display the results in an easily understood way for use in managerial decision making. This includes a well-defined set of metrics against which performance can be measured.

- Robust supplier relationship and category management processes to identify, monitor, and control both critically required materials and the suppliers who provide them.

- An IT infrastructure that enables upstream and downstream communication across the global supply chain network. The system needs to provide timely, transparent information throughout the chain of supply regarding scheduling changes, transportation delays, and any potential event that could disrupt the supply chain's activities.

Risks are not static; therefore, the system used to manage them must be flexible enough to accommodate variability. Supply chain professionals must constantly evaluate and appraise conditions in the environment for signs of new risks or changes in risks already identified. It is a never-ending task.

Examples of Supply Chain Events and Consequences

The need for effective supply chain risk management was particularly illustrated by a series of events in 2007.

NAFTA

In March of 2007, Mexico issued a list of U.S. products that would be subjected to tariffs. Under the terms of the *North American Free Trade Agreement* (NAFTA), tariffs were supposed to be eliminated between the United States and Mexico. However, the Mexican government was upset that the United States had failed to meet its NAFTA obligations by refusing to allow Mexican trucks into the country. The consequence was an unexpected cost for U. S. firms that exported certain products to Mexico..

- *Source of risk*—Government regulations
- *Consequence*—Disruption in the supply chain to Mexico and increased costs for U.S. businesses and Mexican consumers
- *Causes*—Lack of U.S. government action in reaching a mutual accommodation with Mexico on the rules for trucks crossing the border

Toys

Companies in China manufacture the majority of all toys sold in the United States. During the years 2006 and 2007, there were numerous recalls of toys sold by Mattel Inc. worldwide. Chinese companies got the blame for the recalls because of issues such as the use of lead-based paint on some toys.

Paint was a problem, but the majority of the toys were recalled because of design defects, not necessarily poor craft or lack of attention to specifications. The safety problems associated with the use of magnets in new toy designs had not been properly addressed. The magnets came loose and were a choking hazard for children.

- *Sources of risk*—Supplier management, product design and specifications, quality assurance processes and procedures

- *Consequences*—Children were exposed to toxic lead and the possibility of choking on broken toy parts. Mattel was forced to recall millions of toys that had been sold all over the world. The company suffered huge financial losses and damage to its brand. Even Chinese manufacturers not involved in the manufacturing of the recalled toys suffered the effects of damaged reputations and loss of business.

- *Causes*—Insufficient supplier relationship management processes that did not include second- and third-tier suppliers; lack of attention to safety needs in new product development; and lack of proper quality assurance and control methods at both supplier locations and at Mattel

Pet Food

Melamine is a chemical commonly used in plastics and adhesives that has been found to be a potential cause for kidney failure in animals and humans. In 2007, well over a hundred brands of pet food were recalled because of possible melamine contamination. As a result of the contaminated food, pets, and in particular cats, died of kidney failure in the United States. The source of the problem was gluten, an ingredient in the pet food that had been contaminated with melamine.

Gluten is a high protein substance made from processed wheat. The gluten had been imported from China, where its level of protein content in part determined its price. Adding melamine to gluten before it was tested resulted in a falsely higher reading for protein content. Chinese suppliers had sent contaminated gluten shipments to U.S. pet food producers in order to increase the prices they were paid for it. Costs to the pet food industry were great as was the emotional pain to those who lost their pets.

- *Sources of risk*—Supplier management, quality assurance and control, fraud
- *Consequences*—Animals suffered painful deaths from kidney failure. Many brand name products were recalled, which not only cost the companies money but also seriously tarnished their image.
- *Causes*—Insufficient supplier relationship management processes; lack of quality assurance procedures at the supplier level and incoming inspection procedures at the pet food producers; illegal and unethical behavior on the part of the Chinese suppliers' personnel

Automobiles

More recently, even sophisticated firms such as Toyota Motor Corporation have encountered problems that made the company reassess its supply chain risk management operations. Toyota has built a brand reputation based upon quality and reliability. That image was tarnished by a series of recalls for defects related to brake and air bag components provided by its suppliers. These problems resulted in recalls that cost the company many billions of dollars and damaged its quality reputation. The situation caused the firm to reevaluate its supplier oversight methods and entire quality assurance system.

However, the event that triggered the most significant change in Toyota's operations was the April 2011 Fukushima earthquake. The quake massively damaged suppliers' facilities, particularly those of electronics component manufacturers in northeast Japan. Toyota's production capabilities were affected worldwide, and output dropped by about two-thirds immediately after the quake.

The economic impact to Toyota was tremendous, but it awakened everyone to the frailty of modern supply chains. What it showed was that problems for even the smallest supplier could have a devastating effect throughout the chain of supply. As a result in 2012, Toyota announced its intention to build an "earthquake proof supply chain." By 2013, the company had made progress toward that goal. The company's actions included:

- Mapping the entire supply chain
- Locating the 1,500 sites responsible for Toyota's components
- Identifying 300 that were single-source locations that presented risk
- Asking suppliers to spread production to multiple locations, hold extra stock, or buy parts from another supplier

- The company's plans also include further consolidation of similar parts to provide suppliers with economies of scale and the development of increased use of common components across its product lines

The four cases described above are just a few examples of failure in supply chain risk management methods. What they should confirm is that risk for the smallest and the largest members of supply chain networks must be identified and controlled. The cost and effort to do so is great, but the consequences of not doing it are greater.

Still Struggling

Let's put the risk management process in a familiar context. Suppose you have saved up for a long awaited vacation to a distant international location. Consider how you would approach risk analysis for the trip.

You would gather the information needed, identify sources of risk, assess any risks discovered and categorize them, determine what action is suitable for the level of each risk, and then take the actions needed. You would probably also continue to monitor the situation for any changes.

1. **Analyze the internal and external environment**

   Your initial step would be to find information that will answer several questions:

   - How much money do I have?
   - How much vacation can I take?
   - Where are the best places to go?
   - How much will it cost to go to each of them?
   - What are the legal issues to consider for any destination?
   - Will my neighbor feed my cat and watch the house?

2. **Identify sources of risk**

   - *Specifications*—The choice of location must satisfy your personal needs.
   - *Financial*—The costs for some destinations would stretch the budget.
   - *Employment*—The boss may not give you all the days off that you need.
   - *Transportation*—Airline flight availability and cost could affect your budget or your schedule.
   - *Legal*—Some destinations will require you to have a valid passport and a visa. This could delay your trip.
   - *Operations*—An unreliable person might not feed your cat and watch the house. The health of the cat or security of your belongings could be at risk.

3. **Assess and categorize sources of risk**

   High risk
   - Approval of vacation days
   - Passport and visa requirements

   Medium risk
   - Choice of destination
   - Budget constraints
   - Airline schedules

   Low risk
   - Person to watch the cat and house

4. **Determine appropriate action**
   - *Approval of vacation days*—Eliminate by convincing the boss that your duties will be fulfilled by the time you leave and you have more than enough available vacation days.
   - *Passport and visa requirements*—Eliminate by choosing a location that requires only your valid passport and does not require a visa.
   - *Choice of destination*—Mitigate by evaluating possible destinations and choosing the one most likely to meet your expectations.
   - *Budget constraints*—Avoid any potential financial problems by evaluating a total cost for the alternatives and choosing one from those that fit within the budget.
   - *Airline schedules*—Mitigate by booking with airlines that have alternate flights available should there be delay or cancellation.
   - *Person to watch the cat and house*—Accept because your neighbor is your best friend whose reliability has been demonstrated over the years.

   You will also have contingency plans for any risk that is subject to change such as flight schedules or significant weather events.

5. **Implement plans**
   - After considering the actions needed, you set out to do them.

6. **Monitor**
   - Before your trip, you will stay on top of weather conditions, flight schedule changes, and any possible event that might prevent your friend from watching the cat.

The result will be peace of mind during an enjoyable trip that didn't shatter your finances. A supply chain risk management process is more detailed and complex but the logic is similar. Find out what the risks are and plan how to control them and then do it. That's not rocket science; just diligent, thorough, hard work.

Summary

Many variables exist in a complex global supply chain network that can disrupt its ability to meet its goals. A supply chain risk management system must be in place to avoid the negative consequences of events that will or might happen. The best risk management systems are developed and implemented from a total supply chain perspective. Having such a system requires an integrated approach to the identification and management of risk that includes all key supply chain members and fosters collaboration internally and externally.

To be effective, the risk management system must have a clear structure and well-defined processes. It must be able to identify possible sources of risk, categorize and prioritize them, assess and implement appropriate measures to manage risk, and continually monitor, report, and act upon changes in the environment.

QUIZ

1. No firm can operate _____ today.
   A. independently
   B. in China
   C. for long
   D. machines

2. _____ strategy is dependent upon the type of risk exposure to be managed.
   A. Short-term
   B. Risk management
   C. Long-term
   D. Inventory

3. _____ risks are the consequences of events that happen without our consent.
   A. Small
   B. Everyday
   C. Dangerous
   D. Involuntary

4. _____ differences can have an impact on negotiations and labor relations.
   A. Time
   B. Domestic
   C. Environmental
   D. Cultural

5. Supply chain management requires _____ risk taking.
   A. no
   B. heavy
   C. some
   D. much

6. Existing or proposed changes in laws, trade agreements, and tariffs are _____ risks.
   A. bad
   B. political
   C. economic
   D. technological

7. Changing public perceptions are _____ risks.
   A. social
   B. economic
   C. normal
   D. political

8. A simple _____ can aid in visualizing potential supply chain risks.
   A. picture
   B. map
   C. meeting
   D. video

9. _____disasters, such earthquakes, hurricanes, floods, or drought, are sources of risk.

   A. Frequent
   B. Small
   C. Man-made
   D. Natural

10. To eliminate risk, a firm must remove the potential _____ that would cause a problem.

    A. business strategy
    B. event
    C. goal
    D. personnel

11. A firm may choose to focus its strategy on supply chain capabilities, such as _____, efficiency, agility, or flexibility.

    A. spending
    B. location
    C. speed
    D. production

12. One of the sources of risk in the pet food recall was _____

    A. finicky pets.
    B. supplier management.
    C. seasonality.
    D. distribution.

13. Important factors that influence the choice of a supply chain strategy include the _____ in which the firm exists, the market for products, the variability of demand, and the product life cycle.

    A. location
    B. nation
    C. industry
    D. culture

14. Suppliers who are not _____ may cease operations.

    A. local
    B. financially sound
    C. corporations
    D. registered

15. A sourcing strategy must balance the _____ of different types of purchases.

    A. seasonality
    B. employees' opinions
    C. relative risk and relative value
    D. timing

chapter 8

Supply Chain Performance Metrics

Metrics bring together strategy and implementation. At the executive level, they help assure that objectives are being met while the organization's business strategy is being executed. For supply chain managers, metrics show how well the supply chain network is performing in support of that strategy. As discussed in Chapter 3, the development of a supply chain strategy is a challenging task. Once a strategic plan has been adopted, its implementation is no less difficult. A system must be put in place that will monitor what is going on, compare the reality against a set of targets, and take action to remedy any problems.

CHAPTER OBJECTIVES

In this chapter, you will learn

- Why metrics are important.
- How the term metric is defined.
- How metrics should be chosen.
- What supplier performance metrics are.

- What supply chain performance metrics are.

- Why the use of metrics alone is not the answer to better performance.

Choosing the right set of performance metrics is essential. What gets measured gets attention (and, hopefully, is improved). Measuring the wrong things is wasteful; neglecting to measure important things can be catastrophic. To do it right, a process must be used to create and deploy an effective and efficient performance measurement system. This chapter will review that process along with specific examples of those metrics applied to supply chain performance.

The Importance of Performance Metrics

In a 2004 article for the *Journal of Operations Management*, Steven A. Melnyk, Douglas M. Stewart, and Morgan Swink identified three primary reasons why performance metrics are important: control, communication, and improvement.

1. *Control*—Metrics allow managers "to evaluate and control the performance of the resources for which they are responsible." This control helps focus those resources on what will maintain a competitive advantage over the competition. By creating *key performance indicators* (KPIs), common goals are set for everyone.

2. *Communication*—Metrics communicate performance to internal and external stakeholders. The external stakeholders, in particular, may not know or understand how a firm operates. Properly designed metrics give them a means to see the overall picture of what is happening.

3. *Improvement*—Metrics will shine a light on actual versus expected performance. This information can be used to identify issues and, if necessary, to take appropriate corrective action for improvement. When personnel know what is expected, KPIs create common goals and shared values, which can help improve employee efficiency and morale.

"You can't manage what you don't measure," sums up the reasons why performance metrics are important. This is true at the senior executive level, where the concern is assuring performance to the overall business vision and strategy. It is true at the supply chain management level, where performance in meeting strategic objectives is critical to the firm's success. It is true at the individual employee level, where monitoring how individuals perform to expectations tends to focus attention on what is important (as long as the right metrics are chosen).

Measures, Metrics, and KPIs

As with any business jargon, the terms measures, metrics, and KPIs may often be confusing. A little clarification of how they are applied in this chapter may be useful.

A *measure* is generally a single numerical value. There is no complexity to it. For example, the number of outstanding invoices, the number of approved suppliers, the number of personnel in the logistics department, or the number of parts in the production materials inventory is each a measure. By themselves, these numbers do not tell much about what is going on because there is nothing fundamentally positive or negative about them.

A *metric* is more complex. It is used to monitor how well a business, a function, or a process is achieving the results expected. To find a value for a metric usually entails some type of computation or comparison. Take production materials inventory, for example (parts, assemblies, components, or anything that goes directly into the product). Combining the information about what is on hand at the end of the year along with measures of other factors produces a metric: *inventory turnover*—a measure of the velocity of inventory or how quickly it is moving through the facility. Here is an example:

Assume three measures of value are known:

1. The value of the year-end inventory was $10,000.
2. The value of the starting inventory was $10,000.
3. The total expense for raw material inventory during the year was $100,000.

Using these three measures, the inventory turns are computed as follows:

1. First a number for the average inventory is calculated:
   Starting inventory + ending inventory divided by 2 = average on-hand inventory
   $$(\$10,000 + \$10,000) = \$20,000/2 = \$10,000.$$
2. Next the total inventory expense is divided by the value of the average on-hand inventory.
   $$\$100,000/\$10,000 = 10.$$
3. The average inventory turns for the year was 10.

Of course this was a very simple example, and inventories are never so simple. What the metric alone does not explain is whether "10" is a good, fair, or poor number. The answer is, "it depends." Metrics are useful as a way to evaluate performance, but it is the factors used for comparison that determine the level of that performance. Those factors would vary by industry, company, and the type of inventory measured. It would be terrific for an industrial hardware distributor to turn its inventory 10 times a year. But it would be unacceptable for an automobile manufacturer's raw materials inventory.

Key Performance Indicators

Not all metrics are equal. Some are more important than others. *Key performance indicators* (KPIs) are metrics, but not all metrics are KPIs, as shown in Figure 8-1. Among the many financial or nonfinancial metrics an organization may have, those associated with critical success factors are labeled as KPIs. Sometimes KPIs are considered to be a top-level indicator only. In this view, they should be used exclusively for the assessment of how well performance is aligned with the overall business strategy and goals. But the term KPI is also often applied to the most critical factors that monitor the performance of a department or process.

At the executive level, KPIs need to be directly linked to the organization's strategic goals. At the functional levels, such as marketing, logistics, and supply management, they must connect with essential performance factors in each function's strategy. Of course the purpose of these functional level strategies

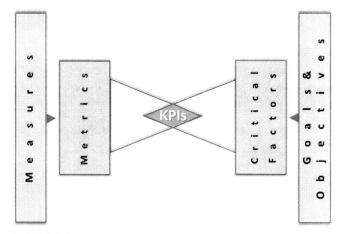

FIGURE 8-1 · KPIs highlight the critical factors for success.

| TABLE 8-1   KPIs: Production Manager versus Retail Executive ||
Production Manager KPIs	Retail Executive KPIs
Defects by worker	Capital expenditures
Time to produce	Store portfolio changes
Labor Hours vs. time to produce	Expected return on new stores
Tools vs. errors	Customer satisfaction
	Same store sales
	Sales per square foot.

is to support the business strategy, as we saw in Chapter 3. KPIs also need to be flexible. While they must not be subject to casual changes, they do need to be modified to reflect an organization's changing goals. Sometimes they must change in reaction to external factors or when the original goals have been achieved.

As Figure 8-1 illustrates, KPIs are the convergence of the critical factors that contribute to reaching the organization's goals and its set of performance metrics. As the term implies, KPIs are the key metrics to be watched.

Among supply chain members, the number and type of KPIs varies significantly. For example, a production manager would need a completely different set of KPIs to keep track of the number of products produced without errors, delays caused by machine downtime, and errors attributable to the production employees, whereas executives in the retail industry want to know how well each store is performing. A comparison of these two sets of KPIs is in Table 8-1, using six retail business KPIs from the 2007 PricewaterhouseCooper's "Guide to Key Performance Indicators."

Performance Targets

Whether or not they are KPIs, one of the characteristics of good metrics is to create them with a target in mind. That means establishing what the metric will be measured against in order to judge performance. Three of these factors for comparison are shown in Figure 8-2.

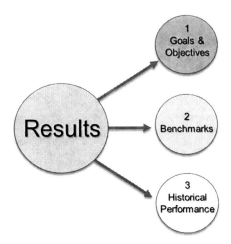

FIGURE 8-2 · Assessing targets for comparison.

Goals and Objectives

As reviewed in Chapter 3, organizational strategy is the means by which the firm's executives intend to fulfill its mission. It is a long-term action plan designed to accomplish broad goals and specific objectives. Strategy establishes the factors that will guide decision making, influence priorities, and allocate the organization's resources. Specific supply chain strategies are guided by the needs of the business strategy. Therefore, not all supply chain metrics are the same, as will be shown later in the chapter.

Benchmarks

Benchmarking compares a firm's operations to those of other organizations. The objective is not to mimic the value of other firm's KPIs but to improve upon them. Benchmarking should not be confined to the firm's own industry either. For example, companies outside of retailing look to the operations of companies such as Amazon and Wal-Mart for logistics benchmarks.

Benchmarking against competitors is also important. Knowing how well the firm is doing against them in areas such as supply chain costs, flexibility, or agility helps to determine the target needed to gain competitive advantage.

History

At the executive level, previous historical measures of financial performance are often used to set targets. For example, *return on assets* (ROA) is one. This is a measure of the return the company is getting from its assets. Past results can also be used at the operational level to set targets for evaluating performance. In supply management, one would be year over year costs of purchased materials as a percentage of total cost of goods sold.

The development, implementation, and monitoring required of KPIs is neither easy nor inexpensive. It is a difficult process that takes time and resources. But once they become part of the way a business operates, the visibility they provide to keep the organization focused will become worth the cost.

 Still Struggling

Sometimes language trips us up. This is one of those times. The terms *measure, metric,* and *KPI* are often used interchangeably. To demonstrate the differences in another way, consider how a supplier is evaluated over time. Usually information is collected for four core factors—quality, cost, delivery, and service—and is then used to evaluate a supplier's performance. A look at the delivery factor is a straightforward way to illustrate how everything fits together.

Number of Deliveries

The number of deliveries a supplier made in one month is simply the measure of all deliveries received during that time. This information is collected along with whether the shipment arrived on time or late. Let's say the supplier made 50 deliveries, as indicated in Table 8-2. These are simply numbers, information that can be used in combination with other data to calculate one or more metrics as follows:

Percent of deliveries made on time—This is a calculation of how many of those 50 total deliveries arrived on time. In this case, 4 were late and 46 were on time. Therefore, 46/50 = 92%. The supplier delivery performance is 92% on time. This percentage is then compared to a target for on-time delivery, say 98%, to judge the supplier's performance.

KPI for individual supplier performance—Supplier delivery performance is one metric that could be rolled in with the three others for cost, quality, and service to create an overall KPI. This KPI would reflect the combined performance results for that supplier, which is an important indicator for use in the SRM methods reviewed in Chapter 4.

> *KPI for combined performance of all suppliers*—The metrics for each supplier could also be rolled together to indicate the combined performance of all suppliers. This result would be valuable information for managers, since it represents how well the supply base is performing. Action would be taken if it indicated downward trends or a lack of improvement on past problem areas.

Characteristics of a Good Metric

In general, when trying to create a set of metrics, anyone can find it difficult to know whether or not a proposed metric is a good one. Questions such as the ones below are common:

- Can the metric be objectively measured?
- Are the expected results clearly defined?
- Is the metric customer focused?
- Are there analysis methods for the metric that can produce meaningful results?
- Are there existing benchmarks for the metric—internally or externally?
- Are the metrics challenging but at the same time attainable?
- What assumptions have been made about the targets for performance

TABLE 8-2 Supplier Delivery Performance

Number of Deliveries		Number On-time		Number Late	
Week 1	12	Week 1	11	Week 1	1
Week 2	13	Week 2	13	Week 2	0
Week 3	11	Week 3	10	Week 3	1
Week 4	14	Week 4	12	Week 4	2
Total	50	Total	46	Total	4

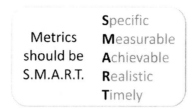

FIGURE 8-3 • SMART chart.

One well-known model to follow in answering these questions is the *SMART* criteria first introduced by George Doran in a 1981 *Management Review* article, as referred to in Figure 8-3. SMART is an easy to remember acronym for the following:

Specific—The definition of the metric must be focused and clear so that everyone can understand it. An income goal that is stated as "I want to make more money" isn't clear. It's vague and not a good starting point in creating a metric. "I want to increase my income as a salesperson by 10% this year" is clear and focused. Income changes can now be measured toward the target of producing a 10% annual increase. To be certain that the metric is understood, include those involved in the activity to be monitored in the development of the definitions.

Measurable—A metric that is quantifiable is best. This means that it can be numerically stated, as it is in the percent of income increase given in the previous "Specific" example. Qualitative metrics, such as "customer satisfaction," need to be analyzed from the perspective of what contributes to them. For instance, completed order fulfillment statistics, number of returns, number of complaints, and warranty claims would be quantifiable results that influence customer satisfaction.

Achievable—Stretch goals are a good thing. Beyond that, however, unachievable or unreasonable goals can discourage rather than motivate.

Realistic—The firm's external environment and the available internal resources need to be assessed to identify any insurmountable constraints. Another sometimes-overlooked issue is the value of what the metric measures. The question to be asked is, "What will knowing that do for us?" If the cost of collecting and analyzing the data is greater than the benefit derived from having it, the metric is not acceptable. Metrics should be confined to only those factors that are genuinely important.

Timely—The time available to reach the objective needs to be a factor in creating metrics. Supply chain cost is a frequent KPI. Setting a target to reduce it by 50% in one year is unrealistic (see the "R" above). The targets for some KPIs are long term, and what the KPI indicates is the progress made toward the long-term goal. In today's business world, performance monitoring needs to be accurate and continual. The collection of data, the analysis, and the publication of the metrics all need to be timely.

Supplier Performance Metrics

Supplier performance is a critical factor in the supply chain's ability to meet its objectives. The three KPIs for supplier performance are those related to quality, cost, and delivery. These factors have to be adjusted according to whether the supplier provides tangible products, such as parts and materials, or services.

KPIs for Product Suppliers

1. *Cost*—Total cost to the firm. Price is the cost element most frequently monitored for changes.
2. *Delivery*—Performance to the schedule. Delivery expectations vary among firms. For automobile manufacturers, it can be quite stringent. Toyota's expectation for delivery was reported by Susan Avery in *Purchasing* Magazine as 100% on-time delivery of the entire order.
3. *Quality*—Compliance to the purchase specifications. The idea that suppliers can have any defective parts is no longer acceptable. The requirement is for virtually defect-free products. This is the Six Sigma approach to quality popularized by GE.

KPIs for Service Suppliers

1. *Contract compliance*—Fulfillment of the contract terms, conditions, and pricing
2. *Customer satisfaction*—How well satisfied the recipient of the service is

Service suppliers are also evaluated on the specific elements in their *service-level agreements* (SLA), which furnish detailed specifications about the service to be provided.

Beyond these KPIs, supplier performance measurement can be multidimensional. A scorecard approach may be used to expand the metrics to other associated areas, such as lead times and cost-reduction efforts. When multiple performance attributes, such as quality, delivery, service, cost, and lead times, are used in a scorecard approach, each of the attributes is assigned a weight, based upon its level of importance. Some may be of greater importance to the firm than others and are weighted accordingly. Doing this helps to avoid distorting a comprehensive score, which could result from giving every attribute the same weight. The result is an integrated performance metric.

Scorecards also detail the criteria used to distinguish between levels of performance, which helps both the buying and supplying organizations. A scorecard requires the buyers to clearly identify which metrics are most important and to measure suppliers accordingly. It provides the supplier with a clear indication of what the focus of performance will be, allows them to align their operations to support it, and provides a feedback loop to help monitor progress and make improvements.

Supply Chain Performance Metrics

The number of supply chain performance metrics both proposed by experts and used by organizations is immense. In fact, the *Supply Chain Operations Reference* (SCOR®) Model alone has 200 KPIs (SCOR Revision 11, 2012). Trying to determine which metrics best fit the previous criteria for being the right one can be a daunting task. There are some considerations that cut across all types of businesses, such as total supply chain costs and customer value added. But the best metrics are those that will focus on the factors most critical in realizing the objectives of the supply chain strategy and the firm's strategic vision and goals.

In the 1991 book, *Keeping Score: Measuring the Business Value of Logistics in the Supply Chain*, James Keebler outlined four very useful categories of metrics for logistics and supply chain performance: (1) time, (2) quality, (3) cost, and (4) other supporting metrics.

1. *Time* has always been considered an essential measure of logistics with on-time delivery/receipt being right at the top. One time metric that Keebler includes is *order cycle time variability*. Monitoring the metric for order cycle time and managing its variability can have great impacts throughout the supply chain. Just a matter of a few days' variability causes inventory requirements to change. The more variability there is, the more investment in safety stocks is required throughout the supply chain network.

2. *Quality* is dominated by overall customer satisfaction. Another quality factor, *perfect order fulfillment*, influences customer satisfaction and is a combined measure of several factors. They include measurements of the on-time delivery of a complete, damage-free order that was accurately invoiced. Keeping track of all these factors is challenging.

3. *Cost* across the supply chain can be a daunting metric to measure. Total delivered cost is another composite metric in this category. It includes the cost of goods, transportation, inventory, and material handling. Additional cost-related factors in the cost category are:

   • *Finished goods inventory turns*—How often the final product inventory is being moved out.

   • *Cash-to-cash cycle times*—A measure of how long the firm's money is tied up in the product until it is sold and returns as cash.

   • *Days' sales outstanding*—How long it takes for the company to be paid after a sale has been made.

   • *Other costs*, such as IT systems and administration, and those resulting from capacity utilization.

4. *Other*—This includes additional factors related to the costs of handling exceptions such as change orders.

SCOR Model Metrics

In the *Supply Chain Operations Reference (SCOR) Model Version 11.00*, the Supply Chain Council identifies Level 1 Strategic Metrics for supply chain management, which are the top-level KPIs. Each Level 1 Performance Attribute indicates "a grouping of metrics used to support a strategy." This statement is consistent with the supply chain strategies that were outlined in Chapter 3. A summary of their recommended attributes, their definitions, and the metrics used to measure performance is shown in Table 8-3.

Essential Characteristics of Supply Chain Metrics

Regardless of which metrics are used, supply chain performance metrics must

   • be tied back to strategy,

   • be developed from the customer perspective,

   • be clear to everyone,

TABLE 8-3 SCOR Metrics		
Performance Attribute	**Definition**	**Level 1 Metric**
Reliability	Right time, quality, quantity	**Perfect order fulfillment** On-time, no damage, and correct documentations
Responsiveness	The velocity of the supply chain activities; how quickly it fulfills customer needs	**Order fulfillment cycle time** The time between when the customer places the order and receives it.
Agility	Responsiveness to external events	**Response time** to unplanned demand
Cost	All costs associated with the supply chain's processes	**Total cost to serve** The sum of all the supply chain cost from beginning to end that are required to fulfill customer demand
Asset Management Efficiency	Effectiveness in managing supply chain assets such as inventory and capacity utilization	This is a measure of three metrics: **Cash-to-cash**[1] **Rerun on fixed assets**[2] **Return on working capital**[3]

Adapted from : Supply Chain Operations Reference Model (SCOR) Revision 11.0

1. Cash to Cash Cycle = [Inventory Days of Supply] + [Days Sales Outstanding] − [Days Payable Outstanding] as measured in days

2. Return on Supply Chain Fixed Assets = ([Supply Chain Revenue] − [Total Cost to Serve]) / [Supply Chain Fixed Assets]

3. Return on working capital = ([Supply Chain Revenue] − [Total Cost to Serve]) / ([Inventory] = [Accounts Receivable]-[Accounts Payable])

- measure what is important, and
- encourage functional collaboration.

Most of these bulleted points were covered previously in the review of the SMART model. Three that merit further comment include:

1. *Tied back to strategy*—This idea has been repeated several times already. Focusing on measures not tied to strategy is self-defeating. "What gets measured gets attention." Focusing the attention of supply chain members on factors that have no strategic impact is a waste of resources.

2. *Developed from the customer perspective*—This is consistent with the first recommendation. As illustrated in Chapter 3, the customer is the focus for strategy development. The strategies that need to be in place create value for the customers in the segments chosen. Speed of delivery in a

TABLE 8-4 Metrics and Consequence

Performance Metric	Consequence
Purchasing: **Purchase Price Variance**	Buyers are incentivized to purchase low-price products. This can actually lead to increasing the total cost of ownership.
Sales: **Orders Booked**	Sales may not reflect production schedules and planned product mix causing added costs for revising the schedule or risk alienating customers.
Engineering: **NPD Time to Market**	Without incorporating design for supply chain, at the beginning, costs of inventory and logistics may be impacted.

segment that cares only about price may not be an appropriate metric. It would be equally inappropriate to have a myopic focus on costs in a segment that highly values speed.

3. *Encourage functional collaboration*—The best outcome would be to have everyone in both the internal and external supply chain onboard with performance metrics. As the later discussion in this chapter on the impediments to metrics will demonstrate, this is a complex and challenging task. However, a firm has the ability to directly control their internal metrics. Internal collaboration is required to create cohesive metrics rather than competitive metrics. Just a few of the consequences resulting from incompatible metrics are identified in Table 8-4.

Take Action

The PDCA cycle introduced in Chapter 7 and seen in Figure 8-4 is a useful tool for getting the most from performance metrics. Planning in the beginning creates the metrics; deploying them is the *do* step; monitoring the metrics is the *check*, and that is not where it stops. The next step is to *act* on the information the metrics provide. Why spend all the time and energy to put a performance metrics system in place if there is no corrective action taken?

Taking action must include the search for and resolution of the cause for the variance between the metric's target and the actual results. This step requires asking questions: Is the metric wrong? Is the target wrong? What interactions

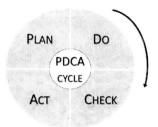

FIGURE 8-4 • PDCA cycle.

with other metrics might have been the cause? Unless the root of the problem is identified and corrected, performance metrics lose their value.

Impediments to Integrated Supply Chain Metrics

Academics and consultants frequently write about supply chain performance. Some themes are repeatedly discussed as major factors that have hindered an integrated approach to monitoring and measuring this performance. Some of these factors are listed below:

- Incompatible goals and objectives among members of the supply chain
- Distrust between supply chain members
- Costs for implementing supply-chain-wide performance measures are not shared
- Individual company strategies require different metrics
- Metrics are not standardized across the supply chain
- Supply chain metrics are all internally focused
- Insufficient or incompatible information technology

Another drawback to using metrics is that they are primarily retrospective. That is, they show what was happening, not what is likely to happen. Past performance is a predictor of future results, but it does not guarantee it. As the discussion on risk in Chapter 7 illustrates, relying on past performance can be a serious deficiency for managers trying to anticipate likely changes in the environment. A best practice would be for firms to identify critical internal and external factors that have the potential to cause harm and then to create a timely system with the most applicable, forward-looking metrics to monitor what is coming.

Technology as a Facilitator

In many firms, the only way to collect the data necessary for metrics is to extract it manually from the separate functional areas because there is no central data repository for the entire firm. Not only may the data be dispersed, it can also be in multiple formats such as Excel worksheets individually adapted from different perspectives by each department. These factors make it challenging to find an easy way to collect and interpret the information and its cross-functional implications.

For example, the accounting department has a vendor database that stores information about any individual or company that does business with its firm. That database can be loaded with cross-listed suppliers who are represented in different ways. One company alone could be identified separately by locations, business units, or the name used to set up the company in the database. This system makes it difficult to extract information that the supply management group would use to monitor performance in relation to the strategic sourcing objectives, as discussed in Chapter 3.

One way to overcome this problem is to have an integrated performance indicator system. Many large and small software systems are readily available for this purpose. Such systems will allow analysis of different KPIs across the company with the ability to then put the information into a useful context that accounts for the interactions across functional boundaries.

Dashboards

An electronic dashboard is similar to the one in an airplane or a car. The instruments on a dashboard display what is happening with the machine's various systems. A metrics dashboard provides a real-time visual display of performance indicators that are used to monitor the firm's operations and drive changes when necessary. In techspeak, a dashboard is a *graphical user interface* (GUI). What it does is collect and display information regarding selected KPIs from across the company. These displays are user-friendly and can be customized to meet the needs of the particular user. Some also provide a way to dig deeper into the underlying information for the data and analysis behind the metrics displayed.

Enhancing the Value of Supply Chain Performance Metrics

Historically, a firm's metrics have been centered on financial performance. Measures such as gross profit and net profit margins as indicators of profitability or working capital as a measure of the firm's financial health and ability to meet any short-term obligations have been center stage in the lineup of what to look at. For supply chain management, and other operational aspects of the company, that focus has been a problem. The focus has been on measures of the outcome without providing a clear understanding of the operational factors that drive the outcome.

Beyond the short-term metrics of financial performance is the long-term ability of any firm to compete. The performance of the supply chain has a significant financial impact on a firm's bottom line, and senior management should not overlook this. A report published by McKinsey & Company in January 2011, *McKinsey on Supply Chain*, noted that in a survey of well over 600 executives, fewer than 26 percent achieve alignment among their company's functions as part of making supply chain decisions. Additionally, 38 percent reported that the CEO had no or almost no involvement with supply chain strategy. Executive attention to a few supply chain KPIs could help assure the collaborative behaviors that will improve the value of the firm's supply chain network.

Summary

Metrics are what bring together strategy and implementation. Therefore, it is important to choose the right set of performance metrics. "You can't manage what you don't measure," and metrics will provide a means to control, communicate, and improve performance. Metrics monitor whether or not a business, a function, or a process is achieving the results expected. KPIs are the top-level metrics, and among supply chain members, the number and type of KPIs varies significantly.

The best metrics are created with a target in mind—one that is based on the firm's goals, benchmarking, or past performance. In creating metrics, using the SMART model is a good way to start while keeping in mind that supply chain performance metrics must

- be tied back to strategy,
- be developed from the customer perspective,
- be clear to everyone,
- measure what is important, and
- encourage functional collaboration.

The number of proposed supply chain performance metrics is immense. An excellent resource for them is the SCOR Model, or choose other model formats, such as the one suggested by James Keebler, which focuses on the dimensions of time, quality, cost, and other factors. The best metrics are those that focus on the critical factors needed to execute the supply chain strategy and support the firm's strategic business vision and goals. Executive awareness of a few supply chain KPIs could help ensure that attention is paid to the metrics that will best drive collaborative behaviors and improve the value of the firm's supply chain network.

The next chapter reviews perspectives on supply chain management's role in accomplishing the goals of a firm's *corporate social responsibility* (CSR) efforts.

QUIZ

1. Three primary reasons why performance metrics are important are _____
   A. cost, quality, and delivery.
   B. time, effort, and cost.
   C. control, communication, and improvement.
   D. communication, lead times, and prices.

2. _____ is generally a single numerical value.
   A. A process
   B. A measure
   C. A goal
   D. An objective

3. _____ are metrics but not all metrics are _____
   A. Outcomes / outcomes.
   B. Numbers / numbers.
   C. Measures / measures.
   D. KPIs / KPIs.

4. One characteristic of good metrics is that they are created with a _____ in mind.
   A. target
   B. supervisor
   C. product
   D. problem

5. _____ compares a firm's operations to those of other organizations.
   A. Hallmarking
   B. Projection
   C. Benchmarking
   D. Analysis

6. A metric that is _____ is best.
   A. valueless
   B. vague
   C. undefinable
   D. quantifiable

7. An acronym for a model to follow in choosing the criteria for metrics is _____
   A. STOP.
   B. SMART.
   C. SIMPLE.
   D. PDCA.

8. The three KPIs for _____ are those related to quality, cost, and delivery.
   A. marketing
   B. executives
   C. employees
   D. supplier performance

9. Regardless of which metrics are used, supply chain performance metrics must be _____
   A. short term.
   B. simple.
   C. tied back to strategy.
   D. based on supplier demands.

10. _____ is a tool that can facilitate the use of metrics.
   A. A form
   B. Technology
   C. A stopwatch
   D. A threat

chapter 9

Corporate Social Responsibility

Corporate social responsibility (CSR) is primarily a philosophy. It is the idea that business has obligations to the world outside a firm's four walls. There is no universal definition for CSR or a consensus about how businesses should engage in it. CSR is also controversial. There are both enthusiastic proponents and ardent opponents who passionately defend their beliefs. Differing opinions about the fundamental purpose and role of corporations separate these two groups.

CHAPTER OBJECTIVES

In this chapter, you will learn

- Background regarding the evolution of today's CSR concepts.
- The most widespread elements of CSR, including sustainability.
- Perspectives for and against the philosophy.
- How CSR initiatives impact supply chain management.
- From examples, what companies are doing.

CSR Background

The notion that businesses have obligations beyond creating products and providing services that generate profit for their owners is not new. The philosophies behind "Corporate Social Responsibility" have existed for centuries, but the phrase itself probably entered the language of business in 1953 with the publication of Howard R. Bowen's book *Social Responsibility of Businessmen*. Bowen identified those responsibilities as "the obligations of businessmen to pursue those policies, to make those decisions, or to follow those lines of action which are desirable in terms of the objectives and values of our society."

While the concept has been around under various names for a long time, the application of CSR practices to supply chain activities is fairly recent. CSR initiatives that are focused on the supply side of the supply chain have increased substantially over the last decade. In fact, sourcing and supplier management methods based on CSR principles are now common. This chapter is a modest attempt to objectively review CSR from various points of view, clarify its importance to supply chain management, and highlight the actions that different firms have taken to implement it.

People, Planet, and Profit

Today CSR is most often viewed as a self-regulated method by which profit-making organizations voluntarily integrate the ethical, social, and environmental interests of all stakeholders in their business decisions, operations, and objectives. Stakeholders are those who are affected by a firm's decisions and operations. They include not only customers but also investors, employees, suppliers, local communities, governmental entities, and society at large.

In general, CSR also includes the obligations these organizations have to protect the environment and benefit the societies within which they exist. Organizations that engage in CSR activities often broaden their performance assessments to include metrics for meeting stakeholder interests. Instead of a singular focus on financial results, they use a method known as the *triple bottom line*. This provides a framework for measuring performance as a balance of social, environmental, and financial outcomes. Also referred to as the 3Ps of people, planet, and profit, the foundation of the triple bottom line is the idea that it is in an organization's best interests to consider its impact on society, the environment, and economic viability. Here is a brief review of what that means:

1. *Social responsibility (people)* relates to a firm's obligation to be a good corporate citizen in both its local community and wherever it conducts business. Among many other duties, this includes providing a safe working environment for employees and compensating them fairly. It means that a firm has a responsibility to hire and promote without discrimination. It requires that suppliers be evaluated to ensure that they operate with proper working conditions and do not use child labor.

2. *Environmental duties (planet)* relate to the ways in which the company practices environmental stewardship—that is, how it manages the impact it has on the environment for the benefit of everyone. This would include preventing pollution, investing in renewable resource management, and eliminating waste throughout the supply chain.

3. *Economic viability (profit)* relates to a firm's responsibility to stay profitable. Balancing the other two responsibilities with this in mind is the key to making CSR efforts successful. No one benefits if a firm endangers its ability to profit and grow from its activities.

CSR Definitions and Obligations

There are many labels for the set of obligations or concepts similar to CSR. How many? Well, it depends. Figure 9-1 includes some of those heard in discussions

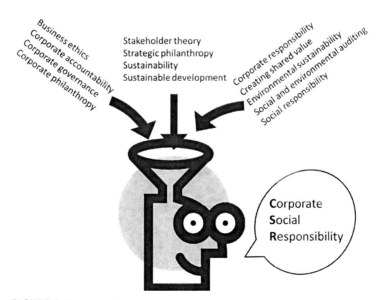

FIGURE 9-1 · Labels for CSR obligations.

with business executives or found in related articles. It is somewhat common to see similar CSR definitions and practices within industry sectors such as automotive or electronics. However, there appears to be neither a universal definition for it nor a consensus about which activities should be included in it.

Sustainability

One CSR component that is often addressed separately and deserves special recognition is that of *sustainability*. A frequently cited definition for the term is found in the 1987 United Nation's *Report of the World Commission on Environment and Development: Our Common Future*, which was written under the chairmanship of Gro Harlem Brundtland:

> *Sustainable development is development that meets the needs of the present without compromising the ability of future generations to meet their own needs.*

How sustainability is defined by individual businesses remains inconsistent, but like CSR, the concept isn't new. Humans long ago realized it was in their best interest to protect the environment that supported their existence. From farmers to fishermen, many who relied on nature for their living learned how to maintain their resources. Unfortunately, these practices were not universal. As the world's population grew and the industrial revolution brought greater demand for raw materials, the results included polluted waterways, smoke-filled air, and deforested hillsides. Nature was to be used up for profit—not sustained for future generations.

The developed world has made progress toward sustainability during the latter half of the last century, but the need for sustainable production is even greater today than it was a century ago. The emerging nations of the world are still finding it difficult to balance their immediate needs for resources and revenue against their long-term need to sustain the environment. With a global population of over seven billion people, sustaining our environment and resources is not optional—it is imperative. To support continuously growing demand in emerging markets, businesses must be a partner in sustainable practices. In this chapter those practices will be reviewed under the umbrella of CSR.

Sustainability Challenges

The need to implement sustainable practices seems evident; however, it is not without challenges for the companies that try to do it. Three of these challenges involve costs, quality, and capital.

1. *Costs*—Companies that use sustainable production practices must still compete with those that do not. Unless there is an evident consumer preference, companies must either be able to minimize the costs of going green (conserving gas, recycling, increasing sustainability, and so on) or lose sales. The use of biofuels is a way to reduce oil dependency and noxious emissions—except that it diverts farm production from human and animal foods into fuel production. It also raises the price of food products globally for their producers and their consumers.

2. *Quality*—If sustainable alternative materials do not meet the customer's quality expectations, there won't be a market for the product. Using green adhesives in cabinetry plywood sounds like a great idea. However, if the glue doesn't withstand the humidity and temperatures of a kitchen, cabinet makers will have unhappy customers.

3. *Capital*—Any capital expenditure must be supported by a business plan that demonstrates a return on that investment. Investment in energy efficiency to conserve resources or minimize emissions must also be balanced to include the cost of the equipment to do it. For many firms, the combined capital and use costs of conventional coal or petroleum systems are still less than those of alternative energy sources.

Sustainability and Supply Chain Integration

In a well-regarded 2009 article for the *Harvard Business Review*, lead author Ram Nidumolu, CEO of InnovaStrat, outlined five stages in the creation of a sustainable supply network:

1. View compliance as opportunity.
2. Make value chains sustainable.
3. Design sustainable products and services.
4. Develop a new business model.
5. Create next-practice platforms.

According to Nidumolu, a total supply chain perspective is essential. Sustainable practices must be incorporated into all supply chain processes: design, sourcing, manufacturing, logistics, and disposal.

Designers should evaluate the manufacturing and packaging materials. Possible end-of-life or remanufacturing uses along with recycling and disposal options should be considered. Suppliers must be evaluated for their capability to meet sustainable standards and comply with environmental regulations. Throughout manufacturing and logistics operations, waste reduction, energy sources, and pollution prevention must be addressed. Transportation and distribution must be planned and scheduled for maximum efficiency, which includes utilizing conservation methods and alternative fuels.

The Buyer's Role in Waste Reduction

Chapters 2 and 4 covered the tactical and strategic roles of supply management. One role concerned supply chain participation in decisions regarding the specifications for purchased materials, goods, or services. When buyers use a TCO perspective for comparisons of purchase options, they can also fulfill a CSR objective of waste elimination.

Consider the purchase of a motor. The initial price paid for that motor represents only part of its total cost. Of greater concern should be the costs associated with running and maintaining it over time. In this instance, paying a higher price for a more efficient motor will reduce energy consumption (reduce waste) in addition to reducing the TCO for the company.

Primary CSR Obligations

One useful framework for discussing CSR was created by Archie B. Carroll. His model includes four categories of responsibility that form the essence of CSR. A representation of the model is illustrated in Figure 9-2 in a pyramid format similar to that originally presented by Carroll in 1991. The model outlines four individual obligations of business in a CSR context. Each obligation is identified independently, but they are all interrelated and sometimes in conflict. That is the paradox that managers face in trying to balance all the obligations in order to achieve CSR objectives.

Economic Responsibilities

Making a profit is essential for businesses. Without profits, any other responsibilities they may have would be irrelevant. Without money, there would be no way to meet those obligations. Business organizations have traditionally been part of the social fabric in their communities. Their principal role in society has been to provide goods and services required by the community and to make a profit in doing so. Just as other members of the community have responsibilities to the societies that support them, so do businesses. A

Responsibilities in each category:

Voluntarily act in a manner consistent with public expectations for corporate philanthropy regarding education and the arts. This applies to the firm itself and its employees.

Demonstrate integrity which includes being a good corporate citizen. This goes beyond just legally required mandates and includes prevailing societal norms for ethical behavior.

Comply with all applicable government laws. A firm must be a law-abiding producer whose goods or services meet at least the minimum legal standards required.

Remain profitable to stay in business and maximize returns to shareholders. To do that a firm must be competitive and efficient

Adapted from the work of Archie B. Carroll, *The Pyramid of Corporate Social Responsibility: Toward the Moral Management of Organizational Stakeholders*, Business Horizons, July-August 1991

FIGURE 9-2 • The pyramid of corporate social responsibility.

singular focus on maximizing profits cannot be an excuse for not fulfilling those obligations.

Legal Responsibilities

Societies establish laws and regulations to organize and clarify the rules regarding what is acceptable and unacceptable behavior for their members. As members of their societies, businesses have an obligation to fulfill their principal role and make a profit doing so within that legal framework.

Ethical Responsibilities

Ethics are societal norms regarding what is fair and reasonable. Some of these norms are the foundation for laws and regulations. Many are not. Just because something is legal doesn't make it right. Society has an expectation that its acceptable standards of conduct are followed by all. Since these standards often vary both within and between different communities, adherence to them can be a particular challenge for business.

Philanthropic Responsibilities

Society expects businesses to do things for its benefit beyond just providing goods and services. Doing so is not a matter of ethics but a demonstration of good corporate citizenship. Wealthy individuals are expected to support the arts, education, and civic events. As members of society with financial and other resources, businesses are expected to behave in the same way, although such actions do not replace other responsibilities. Philanthropy is the ultimate voluntary act that highlights business efforts to be good citizens in returning something to the community above what the law and ethics requires.

Just as the triple bottom line is only a framework for assessing the success of a firm's CSR efforts, Carroll's pyramid is only a guide for identifying a firm's duties in regards to CSR. Neither model identifies the specific activities required nor exactly how the outcome of those activities is to be measured. The activities a firm chooses to undertake and the methods its management uses to evaluate its success vary widely. In general, those firms that best embrace the CSR philosophy incorporate it into their strategies and identify ways to implement it that are consistent with their core mission and purpose. The simplest way to illustrate this is with specific examples of various industry practices and the way results are measured. Later in the chapter, we will do just that.

Perspectives for and against CSR

CSR can be a divisive topic. Any discussion about it is based upon an individual's beliefs regarding the obligations of business beyond profit making and, if such obligations exist, how to fulfill them. Is doing good for everyone a firm's responsibility? If so, exactly what is included in that responsibility? How should a firm go about meeting those duties? The questions raised by both those who support CSR and those who oppose it are not easily answered. Looking at CSR from both points of view helps to understand the dilemmas it creates.

Proponents of CSR

Arguments that favor CSR usually fall into one of two categories: those based on ethical considerations and those that rely upon economic factors. From an ethical perspective, proponents view businesses as part of society, not apart from society. Society is a group of humans who live together in an organized community. A business is operated by humans. All members of the society, including those in business need to act in accordance with the ethical norms of that society. Therefore, business should be no exception. A business operates within a community and derives its revenues and labor from that community.

It benefits from the infrastructure the community provides, such as access to water, power, and transportation. Police, fire, and emergency services are also available and financed by the community at large. From an economic perspective, proponents point to the benefits a firm derives from CSR activities, which can include a positive public image, improved employee recruitment and retention opportunities, and brand enhancement.

Some other claims made in support of CSR include the following:

- CSR can reduce the risk of negative events, such as the 2013 disaster in Bangladesh that led to a general outcry against apparel firms or the continuing problems for electronics companies related to contract manufacturers in China. These events are related to the issue of risks as discussed in Chapter 7, and their consequences might have been avoided had there been more attention given to CSR in supply management.

- Public opinion favors elements of CSR, such as sustainability, transparency, and concern for labor equity throughout the supply chain.

- CSR restrains the growth of government regulations by reducing the need for legislation to address social and environmental issues. Implementing CSR may also help firms avoid having to introduce costly compliance measures that result from new statutes.

- Profitability is boosted when customers and communities have a positive attitude toward businesses that demonstrate concern for CSR objectives.

- The value of the corporate brand, and thereby shareholder equity, is improved through public awareness of a firm's CSR efforts. The value of a brand is something to be protected. CSR initiatives proactively reduce the likelihood of incidents that may damage a brand.

- Environmental degradation has an impact on everyone, including business people and shareholders. It can ultimately affect the availability of resources required by the business. The need for conservation to protect ocean fisheries is an example.

- Ethical behavior is expected of individuals and the businesses they run.

CSR Opponents

Opinions regarding the primary goal of a business are the foundation for many arguments against CSR. Critics of CSR argue that maximizing shareholder value is the main purpose of business; anything that distracts from or dilutes efforts toward that end is unacceptable. The 1919 landmark Michigan Supreme

Court decision in *Dodge v. Ford Motor Company* is frequently held as support for that perspective. Henry Ford had wanted to reinvest profits in the business for the stated purposes of increasing employment and helping workers improve their lives. (His actual motives have been widely questioned.)

John and Horace Dodge were investors in Ford's company and demanded that profits be distributed as dividends. They sued Ford and the case ultimately wound up at the Michigan Supreme Court. In part, that court's decision stated that a corporation must be managed for the benefit of its shareholders. It is claimed that this decision helped solidify the perspective that the primary obligation of a business is to maximize profit for its shareholders.

The late economist Milton Friedman is one of the most widely quoted opponents of CSR who supported this idea. He forcefully argued that CSR undermines the ability of a business to meet its core responsibilities of maximizing profits and shareholder value. However, Friedman's support of corporate profit making was not unconditional. He also said that a corporation's pursuit of profit must be done in compliance with society's laws and ethical customs. (Interviews with Milton Friedman on this topic can be readily found on the Internet.)

More than thirty U.S. state governments have enacted corporate constituency statutes that reduce the effect of the Michigan Court's decision. These laws specifically allow corporate boards of directors more latitude in their decisions about the distribution of profits. The statutes provide them with the freedom to consider the interests of persons who are not shareholders in the corporation. As defined before, the stakeholders may include employees, customers, suppliers, and the local community.

Some of the claims made in opposition to CSR include the following:

- The goals of CSR are inconsistent with the essential profit maximizing goal of business. Attention paid to CSR initiatives diverts resources from a firm's principle objective of maximizing profit.

- The costs of CSR must be absorbed from profits or passed on to customers as higher prices. This reduces returns to shareholders and may hinder the firm's ability to provide competitive pricing in a market.

- Business managers are skilled at managing businesses not social programs. The managerial resources of a firm are expenses that are best utilized in pursuit of the firm's primary objective—profits.

- Business managers are not accountable to the public at large for the success or failure of their CSR efforts. Since by their nature CSR efforts are voluntary and lack enforcement, the public cannot penalize managers for unsatisfactory outcomes.

- Customers don't demand it. Customers are mainly price driven and will oppose increases caused by the costs associated with CSR activities.
- CSR efforts are nothing more than investments in public relations. Shareholders are better served by directing publicity funding toward the more effective methods of influencing customer perceptions.

Skeptics

Skepticism about the motives and benefits of corporate CSR efforts is not uncommon even among those who might otherwise approve of its lofty objectives. The nongovernmental organization (NGO) Christian Aid has suggested that CSR is just public relations conducted under the guise of doing good works. From a skeptic's perspective, it's all about enhancing a firm's image in the public mind. Protecting or enhancing the value of the brand is more important than any tangible value created for society or the environment. In fact, the costs of promoting a firm's CSR programs may even exceed those associated with the actual CSR actions undertaken.

Why might the public become cynical about CSR efforts? They might do so when:

- An energy corporation's advertising promotes its efforts in developing green operations, while news reports broadcast its latest oil spill.
- Electronics firms display all the ways their new gadgets improve the quality of life for users, while newspapers show pictures of the workers who make them protesting sweatshop conditions.
- A grain-like crop, quinoa, is heavily promoted as a healthy, nutritious alternative to other plant foods. Consequently, it becomes so popular that demand drives up prices and the poor people who grow it can no longer afford what had been a staple of their diet.

Firms should pay attention to this skepticism and demonstrate the legitimacy of their CSR efforts. Watchdogs will continue to monitor events as they happen, and that isn't bad. As Chapter 8 suggested, what gets measured gets attention. Corporations must "walk the talk" and be transparent about the purpose, goals, benefits, and costs of their CSR initiatives. To do that, they must

- avoid making exaggerated claims about the benefits of what they are doing,

- not engage in frivolous activities where more is spent to advertise what is being done than is spent to do it,

- be aware that any benefit claimed will be challenged, so they should have the data to support it, and

- not do things for publicity value alone. If for no other reason, doing so may have the opposite effect of what was intended—by encouraging negative instead of positive perceptions of the firm.

The CSR Monitors

In terms of revenue, McDonald's is the world's largest fast food restaurant chain with over $24 billion in sales and almost 33,000 locations. Therefore, McDonald's has a huge global network of meat, poultry, and fish suppliers. This makes it a highly visible target for animal rights groups, who closely monitor its buying practices. Any incident of animal cruelty on the part of a McDonald's supplier is quickly publicized. *People for the Ethical Treatment of Animals* (PETA) even hosts a website named McCruelty.com exclusively to expose McDonald's use of suppliers who are deemed guilty of the inhumane treatment of animals.

McDonald's sustainability efforts include monitoring supplier performance based upon efficiency, sustainability, quality, and safety. The company requires suppliers to comply with ethical policies and practices and does act on allegations of animal mistreatment. For example, when an animal rights group found that a McDonald's egg supplier was engaged in the cruel treatment of young chickens, McDonald's dropped the supplier.

Customers and CSR

There seems to be no clear, compelling evidence to support all the claims made by either side in this debate. However, one thing is apparent: customers have a lot to say about the extent to which CSR is incorporated into the strategies and practices of a corporation. When customers demand it, companies will comply. When doing good and making money coincide, it is a win-win result. Retail grocers have started to carry more organic foods because customers want them. Fast food companies have expanded their offerings to include healthier choices. Auto manufacturers continue to improve the energy efficiency of their vehicles. Customers drove those decisions—not good intentions.

Public awareness of which firms engage in CSR has had an impact on buying behavior. Positive brand awareness and protection of brand reputation are always business concerns. To the extent that CSR practices enhance customers' positive perceptions of a firm and help eliminate the causes of negative publicity, the corporate use of CSR practices will continue to grow.

CSR in Supply Chain Management

In the Chapter 3 discussion on strategy and planning, CSR was listed among the many elements to be considered in creating not only the firm's overall strategy, but also the supply chain and supply management strategies. CSR should be part of business planning at all levels in order to ensure that it is consistent with a firm's mission and values and becomes embedded in the culture of the organization. The following section looks at how firms in various industries integrate the philosophy of CSR into their supply chains. In addition to illustrating what firms are doing, these examples will highlight the significant impact supply chain management has in making it happen.

Consumer Products

Procter & Gamble (P&G) is the largest *consumer packaged goods* (CPG) company in the world. In 2007, the corporation launched a comprehensive strategy to improve "environmental and social sustainability." While the initial program had a five-year horizon, P&G recognized that this was a long-term, ongoing effort to embed CSR into its business structure. It included a vision for long-term environmental sustainability: powering plants with 100% renewable energy, using 100% renewable or recycled materials for all products and packaging, and allowing zero manufacturing and consumer waste to end up in landfills.

P&G's strategy embraced all its operations throughout its supply chain. The strategy identified three areas of focus: products, operations, and social responsibility. To achieve the outcomes expected, two other components were included that would enable progress: employees and stakeholders. P&G's original plan identified the following five elements:

1. *Delight the consumer with sustainable innovations that improve the environmental profile of our products.*

   • *Develop and market at least $50 billion in cumulative sales of "sustainable innovation products," which are products that have an improved environmental profile.*

2. *Improve the environmental profile of P&G's own operations.*

  - *Deliver an additional 20% reduction (per unit production) in CO_2 emissions, energy consumption, water consumption, and disposed waste from P&G plants, leading to a total reduction over the decade of at least 50%.*

3. *Improve children's lives through P&G's social responsibility programs.*

  - *Enable 300 million children to Live, Learn and Thrive. Prevent 160 million days of disease and save 20,000 lives by delivering 4 billion liters of clean water in our Children's Safe Drinking Water program.*

4. *Engage and equip all P&G personnel so that they can build sustainability thinking and practices into their everyday work.*

5. *Shape the future by working transparently with our stakeholders to enable continued freedom to innovate in a responsible way.*

P&G summarized its progress in meeting its goals with the publication of the 2012 *Sustainability Overview* report. Below are summary comments drawn directly from the P&G 2012 *Sustainability Overview* report (PDF). They are not direct quotes, but some of the words are, of necessity, the same.

1. *Develop $50 billion in Sustainable Innovation Products (SIPs)*

  - *P&G focuses on their top brands such as Pampers, Tide, and Ariel. Most importantly, the focus of Sustainable Innovation Products is to achieve all this without any trade-offs for the consumer. The company surpassed the goal with over $52 billion in cumulative sales of SIPs.*

2. *Improve the environmental profile of P&G's own operations*

  - *Except for energy and CO_2 emissions, the company met or exceeded their goals. Efforts continue to meet or exceed the goals not reached.*

3. *Improve children's lives*

  - *Both goals were exceeded.*

(The full report, *P&G Report Card: Final Results for 2012 Sustainability Goals* is available on its website, http://www.pg.com/en_US/sustainability/strategy_goals_progress.shtml)

Note that all supporting information is from P&G publications and should be subject to scrutiny. However, the important aspect of this example is that the organization created a strategy, established goals and methods for achieving it, embedded them into its operations, and monitored their progress regularly. The company actively involved both internal and external stakeholders throughout the supply chain. This included its customers, employees, freight carriers, and suppliers, as well as others, such as local governmental agencies. The company was able to improve supply chain performance, while reducing costs and while meeting CSR objectives. The P&G process can serve as a model for other firms.

CSR and NPD: Compatible 3-Letter Acronyms

One of the areas of focus for P&G is the elimination of packaging waste throughout the supply chain. It is important to recognize that these activities are best done early in the process, during the *new-product development* (NPD) phase. As noted in previous chapters, the NPD process is where most costs can be identified and eliminated or reduced. During NPD is also where a CSR perspective can reap great benefits.

Textile and Apparel Industry

The risks apparel companies take by neglecting CSR were evident in the examples presented in Chapter 7. The consequences can devastate a brand when high-profile names are the subject of negative publicity. Consumer backlash is often swift and harsh. Since apparel firms primarily outsource all of their production requirements to textile manufacturers, supplier relationship management is a critical element in meeting CSR objectives.

Hong Kong–based Esquel is one of the world's leading producers of cotton shirts. The company employs over 54,000 people and has production facilities in China, Vietnam, Malaysia, Sri Lanka, and Mauritius. Its vertically integrated operations provide shirts for global apparel brands, such as Ralph Lauren, Tommy Hilfiger, Nike, J.Crew, Brooks Brothers, and Hugo Boss. Sustainability has long been a focus of Esquel's operations. In 2000, Esquel was one of the first textile companies in China to have its production sites certified under the international environmental management standard ISO 14001, and in 2004, it created a formal corporate social responsibility department that reports to the top executive level of management.

Esquel collaborated with Nike to ensure a sustainable supply of organic cotton from China. The two companies partnered with and microfinanced many local Chinese farmers to help them implement new, more sustainable processes. Esquel assisted farmers in adopting drip irrigation systems to decrease water usage, in creating natural pest and disease control programs, and in implementing harvesting techniques that avoid the use of chemical defoliants.

The company also changed its *supplier relationship management* (SRM) methods to create more collaborative partnership-like arrangements with its suppliers. As a consequence of these actions, Nike can boast of better attention to sustainability in its supply chain, and Esquel has become the largest producer of organic cotton in China. This provides Esquel and Nike with a sustainable competitive advantage.

The Electronics Industry

The supply chain costs of packaging include not only the materials used for it but also the impact it has on other elements such as transportation, warehousing, and disposal. Savings of up to 20 percent have been from supply chain packaging cost reduction initiatives. This is one area where CSR and saving money go hand-in-hand, as the following Dell example illustrates. According to Dell, the company's packaging strategy has eliminated over 20 million pounds of packaging since 2008 and reduced costs by more than $18 million.

Dell considers sourcing an important aspect of mitigating packaging costs. By using local and regional sources of supply, the company reduces transportation costs and associated environmental impacts. In addition, the company's investigation into nontraditional packaging materials has resulted in cost savings and satisfaction of CSR objectives. For example, the company uses bamboo pulp as an alternative to molded paper pulp, foams, and corrugated materials. Bamboo is a highly renewable, fast growing plant, and the products made from it are returned to the soil.

Dell has also begun to test the use of a mushroom-based process that creates a material used as a replacement for foam packaging. In this unique and quite innovative technique, otherwise organic waste, such as wheat chaff or the hulls from cotton or rice, are placed in a mold that is injected with mushroom spawn (the "seed" material used to cultivate mushrooms). After a week or two, the mushroom structure has used the energy of the waste material to create a product similar to foam. Besides being made of sustainable materials, the resulting packaging decomposes into a soil amendment. Dell's efforts provide examples of a true closed-loop sustainable process. In this case, fast-growing plants or otherwise scrap materials provide supply chain packaging that can safely return to earth.

These three examples demonstrate that good CSR initiatives which are embedded in corporate strategies and deployed throughout the supply chain can reap great rewards for the companies involved and all their stakeholders.

Summary

Corporate social responsibility (CSR) is primarily a philosophy about the role and obligations that businesses have regarding their stakeholders. CSR is most often viewed as a self-regulated method by which profit-making organizations voluntarily integrate the ethical, social, and environmental interests of all stakeholders in their business decisions, operations, and objectives. Firms that embrace CSR broaden their performance assessments to include metrics for meeting those stakeholders' interests. Instead of a singular focus on financial results, they use a method known as the triple bottom line: people, planet, and profit. Sustainability is a major element in CSR, and according to the United Nations, it means "…development that meets the needs of the present without compromising the ability of future generations to meet their own needs."

CSR is controversial. Those who are for it argue that profit-making organizations have obligations to the societies in which they do business. Those who oppose it argue that the role of business is to maximize profits, not do good works for society. CSR efforts have had mixed results. For some companies there has been both profit and good work. For some, CSR has been more of a public relations effort without benefit to society. There are many examples of compatible goals between CSR and maximizing the efficiency of the supply chain. Since many companies with different CSR agendas (or none at all) form supply chain networks, only through internal and external collaboration in CSR efforts can its benefits be fulfilled.

QUIZ

1. _____ is the idea that business has obligations to the world outside its four walls
   A. Corporate social responsibility
   B. Social awareness
   C. Shareholder equity
   D. People power

2. The triple bottom line measurement refers to the 3Ps of _____
   A. past, present, and future profit.
   B. profits, process, and procedures
   C. people, planet, and profit.
   D. personnel, planning, and projects.

3. _____ are those who are affected by a firm's decisions and operations.
   A. Stockholders
   B. Stakeholders
   C. Competitors
   D. Governments

4. CSR definitions and practices are _____
   A. all the same.
   B. different among industries and companies.
   C. clearly understood.
   D. set by government rules.

5. Businesses have an economic responsibility to _____
   A. compete in the marketplace.
   B. keep the economy going.
   C. support government spending.
   D. make a profit.

6. _____ are societal norms regarding what is fair and reasonable.
   A. Behaviors
   B. Ethics
   C. Laws
   D. Etiquettes

7. From an ethical perspective, businesses may be viewed as a part of _____
   A. the environment.
   B. government.
   C. humanity.
   D. society.

8. Cost, quality, and capital are _____
   A. three business challenges for sustainability efforts.
   B. the main reasons business exit.

C. the most important measures of business success.

D. easily obtained.

9. **Opponents of CSR say the core responsibility of business is to _____**

A. be competitive.

B. decrease operating costs.

C. maximize profit and shareholder equity.

D. provide customer service.

10. **Companies will engage in CSR when _____ demand it.**

A. special interests

B. suppliers

C. customers

D. laborers

11. **Supporters of CSR say it can reduce the risk of _____ publicity.**

A. local

B. widespread

C. biased

D. negative

12. **_____ think CSR activity is all about enhancing a firm's public image.**

A. All people

B. Supporters

C. Skeptics

D. Business managers

13. **_____ backlash is often harsh when companies fail to enforce CSR with suppliers.**

A. Shareholder

B. Customer

C. Government

D. Student

14. **Opponents of CSR say that _____ mainly care about prices and not CSR.**

A. customers

B. shareholders

C. suppliers

D. governments

15. **CSR should be considered when creating _____**

A. dividend payments.

B. business and supply chain strategies.

C. inventory projections.

D. sales forecasts.

chapter 10

The Future of Supply Chain Management

As the previous chapters demonstrated, supply chain management is an evolving discipline. What its future strategies, designs, and processes will be is uncertain. However, one thing is certain—supply chain management will not only persist but will also continue to increase in importance. This brief final chapter looks at some past predictions about supply chain management, ideas about what could happen in the future, and the implications for personal careers.

CHAPTER OBJECTIVES

In this chapter, you will learn

- What globalization is.
- Why some predictions about the future proved to be correct.
- What some factors are that will drive changes in supply chain management.

Rethinking Supply Chain Management

The concept of "supply chain thinking" has been around for a while. As a result, many supply chain strategies were developed and implemented when the global business environment was quite different. In its early days, supply chain management was viewed as more of a cost-cutting tool than as anything else. That perception is changing, and where current trends and future events will take it is unclear. Of course, predicting trends and their future consequences can be a lighthearted exercise—most of the time people will have forgotten whatever was predicted and written years before.

Futurists who author books on the subject are sometimes right. Alvin Tofler, in his book *The Third Wave*, envisioned what we now call the information age: a revolutionary change that would bring humankind many benefits along with the negative effects of "information overload." H.G. Wells was another writer who clearly forecast many future technologies and events in both his fiction and nonfiction works. No one could match the prophetic abilities of those two writers in suggesting the future of supply chain management.

This chapter is a very modest attempt to explore a few issues that drive change and to suggest what those changes might be. It begins with a quick look at some past predictions about supply chain management and continues with a few ideas about forces and factors that will have an impact on the discipline now and in the future. A framework for this will be four of the PESTLE analysis elements reviewed in Chapter 3: political, economic, technological, and environmental. However, the first step will be to consider the most talked about driver of change, globalization.

Globalization

Since it was popularized in the 1980s, the term *globalization* has become the most frequently cited agent of change. What globalization exactly is depends on who defines it. The *International Monetary Fund* (IMF) definition is

> Economic "globalization" is a historical process, the result of human innovation and technological progress. It refers to the increasing integration of economies around the world, particularly through the movement of goods, services, and capital across borders. The term sometimes also refers to the movement of people (labor) and knowledge (technology) across international borders. There are also broader cultural, political, and environmental dimensions of globalization.

As a consequence of globalization and the advance of technology, some authors see the world becoming "flat." This idea was popularized by Thomas L. Friedman in his book, *The World Is Flat: A Brief History of the Twenty-First Century*. Friedman suggests that "ten flatteners," or trends, are creating a "level playing field" across the world. These included changes such as the demise of communism and the global expansion of the Internet. He uses the metaphor of a "flat world" to describe the consequences these changes are producing. (Certainly if the world were physically flat, logistics would be much easier.)

One who disagrees with the idea of a flatter world is Harvard Professor Pankaj Ghemawat. In his book, *Redefining Global Strategy: Crossing Borders in a World Where Distances Still Matter*, Professor Ghemawat sees the world as being in a state of "semiglobalization" that will last for decades. His advice is for companies to "resist a variety of delusions" about how globalization will impact their operations. He recommends looking at the cultural, administrative, geographic, and economic differences around the world and assessing each category before assuming the benefits of a flat-world perspective.

Whichever viewpoint will be proven in the future, it is unquestionably true that the globalized business environment has altered supply chains and their management. For years, there have been predictions about how the future would evolve as globalization continued to shape supply chains and their operations. What follows are some predictions made in two studies several years ago.

The Transformation of Supply Management

Supply management is always seen as one of the critical processes in managing the supply chain network. A landmark study on the future of supply management, *The Future of Purchasing and Supply: A Five and Ten Year Forecast*, was published in 1998 by CAPS Research, . The study found eighteen initiatives that purchasing executives considered major concerns for the future. Some of the key elements in the predictions for each initiative are summarized as follows:

1. *Electronic commerce*—The study predicted that the Internet would become the "backbone of electronic purchasing." Use of the Internet will allow the supply chain to utilize a pull system of replenishment based upon actual sales.

2. *Strategic cost management*—Cost reduction efforts through supply chain collaboration and process improvements will continue to dominate efforts

to blunt competitors' cost advantages. Decision making and metrics will reflect the need to manage costs strategically.

3. *Strategic sourcing*—Supply strategies that provide cost and technological advantage will be used. This will require tighter integration with suppliers, a more robust set of supplier selection and management processes, and robust evaluation and performance metrics.

4. *Supply chain partner selection and contribution*—Selection of suppliers in all tiers will become more important as supply chains become more integrated. The competency of purchasing personnel will be a critical asset as suppliers and buyers engage in joint planning, resource sharing, and product development.

5. *Tactical purchasing*—The tactical aspects of purchasing will become more automated. As a consequence, purchasing departments will remain but with a reduced number of personnel.

6. *Purchasing strategy development*—Supply chain strategies will increasingly influence overall business strategy.

7. *Demand-pull purchasing*—Demand-pull systems will be facilitated by the Internet but are unlikely to be fully implemented.

8. *Relationship management*—As customer and supplier relationships across the supply chain become increasingly important, senior executives will focus more attention on the management of both.

9. *Performance measurement*—The measure of prices paid will continue to be a key metric. However, a set of common supply chain performance metrics based upon business unit strategy will emerge.

10. *Process uncoupling*—A focus on core competencies will drive firms to greater use of outsourcing in which core functions, such as design and development, are retained and processes, such as customer order fulfillment, are outsourced.

11. *Global supplier development*—The recruitment of suppliers in foreign markets will continue, but existing strategic domestic suppliers will be encouraged to expand their capabilities to these offshore markets.

12. *Third-party purchasing*—The use of third-party providers for the purchase of nonstrategic items under blanket agreements will continue to increase. Use of the Internet to deploy the order release process will become common, but the purchasing department will continue its oversight and management of supplier performance.

13. *Virtual supply chain*—For specific markets the creation of virtual supply chains that are based upon short-term legal agreements will continue. Full integration of the members of the supply chain will be difficult to achieve.

14. *Source development*—Facilitated by advances in information technology, the integration of members of the supply chain will continue. Development of new suppliers to replace or augment existing supplier relationships and the full integration of all suppliers into supply chains will remain a challenge.

15. *Competitive bidding/negotiations*—The use of competitive bidding when appropriate will continue particularly for governmental entities.

16. *Strategic supplier alliances*—The development and importance of strategic supplier alliances will continue to increase as firms focus on core competencies and outsourcing expands. These alliances will help create competitive advantages for the firms involved.

17. *Negotiations strategy*—Negotiations will continue to be an important aspect of global supply chain management. The process will increasingly become focused on achieving mutual benefit for the parties involved rather than opportunistic advantage for one side.

18. *Complexity management*—Those firms that dominate their supply chains will greatly influence the suppliers in all tiers. There will be challenges in trying to manage shared technology and resources in a mutually beneficial manner. Supply management professionals will be faced with increasing complexity in the management of supplier relationships.

In retrospect, the authors were perceptive. All of these changes have occurred in the past 15 years. Particularly in large firms, there has been an increasing elevation of supply management's role. Topics covered in Chapters 3 and 4, strategic sourcing and supplier relationship management, represent the increased involvement by supply management in company processes and the types of change that CAPS Research predicted. The skills required to engage in these tasks have also transformed the professional profile of the employees who do them.

Past Perspectives on Challenges Ahead

In 2006, eight years after the CAPS study, the faculty of the Eli Broad College of Business at Michigan State University published, *Supply Chain Management*

2010 and Beyond: Mapping the Future of the Strategic Supply Chain. The authors identified five issues that were judged as those that would be most important in the future:

1. Supply chain disruptions and supply chain risk
2. Leadership within the supply chain
3. Managing the timely delivery of goods and services
4. Managing product innovation by drawing on the capabilities of the supply chain
5. Implementing appropriate technology to allow seamless exchange of information within the supply chain

The five predictions are less specific than the CAPS study, but seven years later they are still among the challenges supply chain management faces. The first one has occurred in numerous recent events, and the fifth is still a major factor that must be dealt with by companies trying to achieve the transparency that supply chain management needs. Although the issues of 2006 are still on the list, the top ones may have changed. In January 2011, McKinsey and Company published the results of a survey conducted among over 600 executives. The two top challenges that the executives saw for supply chain management were (1) increased volatility of customer demand and (2) increased pressure from global competition.

Perspectives on the Future of SCM

Here is where the elements from the PESTLE analysis will help categorize the types of change that might be expected as well as highlight the most prominent sources of both the expected and the unanticipated challenges that lie ahead.

Political

As we saw in Chapter 7, anticipating risk and planning for ways to manage it must be an essential element in supply chain strategy development. Unfortunately, not all sources of risk can be known. For instance, the consequences of political events and governmental decisions can alter the landscape of business overnight. This means that some companies will need to rethink and redesign their supply chains to accommodate the unanticipated changes and emerging challenges. One possible unexpected adjustment identified by the *World*

Economic Forum (WEF) could be to nontariff measures. Such measures are imposed by governments mainly for protectionist or political reasons and can be quickly implemented.

Economic

Many early supply chain strategies were efforts to drive out cost, and many of those involved outsourcing to low-cost countries such as China. Nevertheless, the global business environment has changed and will continue to do so. The BRICS (Brazil, Russia, India, China, and South Africa) are developing closer economic relationships. With 40 percent of the world's population, this huge trading block will need to be accommodated by supply chain management because of the influence it could have on global commerce.

Market opportunities are expanding in these developing economies, while their labor costs are rising. Strategies that have only embraced the use of low-cost labor will need to change. The rationale for where companies locate production can now be a consequence of growing local demand rather than a need to exploit low wage rates. Companies are now manufacturing and sourcing both domestically and offshore.

Technological

The impact of technology on supply chain operations and management has already been enormous. Without the advances of the past two decades, vast global supply networks would not exist. Some areas that will continue to foster change include:

- *Communication*—Enabled by the Internet, the communication and information sharing technologies will continue to grow. The new systems available today have changed the fundamentals of how organizations can be structured. Rather than employing full-time staff, companies can assemble available resources from anywhere in the world on an as-needed basis. Virtual teams may become a large fixture in an organizational structure that includes collaborators from supplier firms.

- *Analytics*—Analytics capable of making sense of big data will improve. Current technology is capable of capturing and storing vast amounts of data. This includes structured data, such as *point of sale* (POS) records and retail loyalty-card transactions, and unstructured data, such as that from social media and web search logs. However, data is meaningless until information can be extracted from it. Firms, such as SAS (originally Statistical

Analysis System) and IBM, along with many others, are actively competing in this space.

Data mining and the use of predictive analytic tools have the potential to vastly improve the accuracy of forecasts—and produce them in almost real time. Once meaningful information can be extracted about trends, market conditions, and consumer behavior, supply chains can potentially be reinvented to be much more responsive.

- *Disruptive innovations*—Disruptive innovations cannot be predicted. They appear and may launch new markets or change the value proposition for existing technologies. The iPad and iPhone relied on improvements in existing microprocessors, miniaturized components, manufacturing, and software, but their introduction altered the landscape for handheld devices.

  The Internet is now mobile, and the ways in which this new customer interface will change business practice have only begun. The consequences will be felt throughout the supply chain as customers locate products, make orders and payments, and demand delivery wherever they are.

- *3D printing*—Additive manufacturing, or 3D printing, has been used to make prototypes for over two decades. It is a process that can create a three-dimensional product from a computer image. While not yet the replicators of *Star Trek* fame, these machines have the potential to replace some commercial production in the future. On an industrial scale, manufacturers may offer Internet-based processes that allow customers to design and create truly individual products.

- *Warehouse management*—Warehouse management will continue to become more efficient through the use of sophisticated software applications and automated storage and retrieval technologies. The increased use of robots and the further expansion of RFID into the supply chain will increasingly transform physical distribution.

Environmental

Demands for corporate social responsibility in labor practices and environmental stewardship are also having an impact on manufacturers and producers. With instant worldwide communications, it's hard for any company to hide from what they or their suppliers are doing. The fallout from poor supplier practices in apparel and consumer electronics has damaged brand reputations and brought renewed calls for companies to improve their CSR and supplier oversight responsibilities. This trend toward greater social awareness and demand for sustainable business practices is expected to grow. Greater emphasis will be given to the sourcing process and supplier relationship practices.

Opportunities for the Future

The complexity and the challenges in managing supply chain networks offer terrific opportunities for those in the field or students seeking a career. Because supply chain management is relatively new, employment titles associated with it are still mainly in functional disciplines, such as warehousing, distribution, and supply management. But things are changing.

Hot New MBA

The June 6, 2013 edition of *The Wall Street Journal* headlined an article by Melissa Korn: "Hot New MBA: Supply Chain Management." The focus of the article was the demand for college graduates with supply chain management degrees and their higher rates of success in finding jobs and getting excellent starting salaries. Companies have begun to realize that the personnel who now manage the supply chain network have primarily shifted over from other areas in the organization. Their backgrounds have usually been tightly aligned with individual functional departments. As new personnel are brought onboard, those with a more holistic perspective are being actively recruited. Colleges and universities are quickly responding to this need.

In January of 2012, *The Association to Advance Collegiate Schools of Business* (AACSB) *International* released a report that showed there has been a marked increase in schools offering undergraduate degrees in supply chain/transportation and logistics. Over the past decade, the number of schools with degree programs in traditional disciplines, such as accounting, banking, and marketing has declined, while those offering supply chain management programs actually increased by more than 40 percent. In addition to university-sponsored degree programs, many community colleges throughout the United States continue to add courses in supply chain management and related disciplines.

As long as there is global commerce, the future for supply chain management professionals will be bright and challenging.

QUIZ

1. The _____ business environment has altered supply chains and their management
   A. shrinking
   B. globalized
   C. compartmentalized
   D. domestic

2. Globalized business has _____ supply management's responsibilities.
   A. decreased
   B. terminated
   C. increased
   D. hindered

3. Many early supply chain strategies were efforts to drive out _____
   A. cost.
   B. time.
   C. quality.
   D. distance.

4. Vast global supply networks would not exist without ____
   A. trucks.
   B. fax machines.
   C. archeology.
   D. advanced technology.

5. Graduates with supply chain management degrees ____
   A. get hired with good salaries.
   B. are paid less.
   C. can't find work.
   D. are declining in number.

Final Exam

1. Supply chain management is _____
    A. of limited value to customers.
    B. another name for logistics.
    C. an important factor in achieving a competitive advantage.
    D. a supplier management technique.

2. What is the term used to describe a method used to maximize the efficiency of the manufacturing process through a reduction in downtime and the raw material, work-in-progress (WIP), and finished goods inventories?
    A. LAME
    B. Lean
    C. QFD
    D. FAST

3. What benefit is there to mapping the supply chain network, its constituent members, and its structure?
    A. It allows marketing to see what's happening.
    B. It allows for the identification of interactions and common constraints that could be sources of risk.
    C. It pinpoints supplier locations.
    D. It provides a visual look at what transportation is needed.

4. When a brewer makes beer, the ingredients in a recipe go through a progressive series of controlled steps. This means the brewer is using what production method?
    A. Project
    B. Discrete
    C. Difficult
    D. Process

5. When is it best to consider the supply chain's design?
    A. Once it's in place so it can be evaluated
    B. Whenever there is a crisis
    C. Right in the beginning when products or services are being developed
    D. At the beginning of every week to stay on top of things

6. Which of the following is *not* a characteristic of supply chain management found in many definitions?
    A. Customer focus
    B. Value-adding processes
    C. Integration and collaboration
    D. Labor savings

7. Early supply chain definitions were focused on _____
    A. getting lower prices from suppliers.
    B. manufacturing.
    C. global business.
    D. departmental functions.

8. The primary function of supply management is _____
    A. to ensure the supply of all the materials, parts, and services required for the firm to produce products and maintain operations.
    B. to ensure the lowest price is always obtained.
    C. to buy cheap parts fast.
    D. to try to outsource all purchases to low-cost countries.

9. Which of the following is true?
    A. There is a specific supply chain model that can be used in any industry.
    B. There is little difference between service supply chains and product supply chains.
    C. Supply chain members must join and pay annual dues to the International Supply Chain Management Association located in New York City.
    D. Supply chains and the management of them vary by industry, markets served, and products and services provided.

10. Negotiators focus on their genuine interests. What is a way to define "interests"?
    A. "Interests" are the buyer's and the seller's positions.
    B. "Interests" are the only right ways of doing something.
    C. "Interests" are the real needs of the buyer and the seller.
    D. "Interests" are what each party can give away.

11. Some authors prefer to use the term "supply chain network" instead of "supply chain" because _____
    A. chains are only as strong as their weakest link.
    B. the network model is linear.

   C. there are many processes, sub-processes, and tasks that involve many intercon-
      nected members at various points in the chain.

   D. the reality of the system more closely resembles a television network.

12. **What type of shipment utilizes a combination of transportation methods?**
   A. Intermodal
   B. Intercity
   C. Intramodal
   D. Crossmodal

13. **Which of the following is *not* a benefit that can be expected from a well-run supply chain management system?**
   A. A competitive advantage
   B. Reduced costs
   C. More inventory
   D. Better customer service

14. **One way to outline the objectives of supply chain management is to use a list commonly referred to as the "7 Rights." Which one of the following was *not* among the seven?**
   A. Right forecast
   B. Right place
   C. Right product or service
   D. Right customer

15. **The segmentation of customers into groups is an important practice because _____**
   A. people like to be grouped together.
   B. the results of the segmentation process influence supply chain strategy and design.
   C. it's easier than looking for offshore market opportunities.
   D. None of these

16. **Three major forces that impact supply chain management are _____**
   A. 1. regionalization; 2. language; 3. culture.
   B. 1. globalization; 2. technology; 3. customer expectations.
   C. 1. U.S. regulations; 2. media; 3. customer expectations.
   D. 1. globalization; 2. technology; 3. advertising.

17. **Supply chain management is important because _____**
   A. global competition forces ongoing efforts to reduce costs.
   B. supply chains have become longer.
   C. customers demand more.
   D. All of these

18. What is often called "stroke of pen" events can change the dynamics of a business overnight. Which of the following is one?
    A. Changes in climate
    B. A change in tariff regulations
    C. Enactment of local traffic laws
    D. Company guidelines for gratuities

19. It can be said that marketing's basic function is to attract and retain customers at a profit.
    A. True
    B. False
    C. Maybe
    D. Sometimes

20. The concept of supply chain management emphasizes _____
    A. collaboration among internal functions.
    B. collaboration with suppliers.
    C. collaboration with customers.
    D. all of the above.

21. What can be said about a customer's perception of "value"?
    A. Everybody has pretty much the same opinion of it.
    B. The same product or service will have the same perceived value in any context or situation.
    C. Customers' perceptions of value cannot be measured.
    D. One of the factors that contribute to customers' perception of value is the context in which they make the decision.

22. The "4Ps" have been expanded over the years. These "7Ps" now often include which one of the following sets of 7 elements?
    A. Product, price, place, promotion, people, process, and physical evidence (packaging/placement)
    B. Practicality, price, place, promotion, people, process, and physical evidence (packaging/placement)
    C. Product, price, place, promotion, people, population, and physical evidence (packaging/placement)
    D. Product, price, place, promotion, people, process, and personal selling

23. If a company lacked the proper equipment or trained personnel to make a product, this could pose serious risks. Which risk strategy might the company use?
    A. Shift the risk to a third party.
    B. Accept the risk and continue to make the product internally.
    C. Defer the risk and stop making the product for a while.
    D. Eliminate the risk by selling the product rights to another company.

24. Regarding packaging, which one of the following statements is *not* true?

    A. Packaging is important because it encloses and protects a product as it travels through the chain of supply.
    B. Two types of packaging are: consumer packaging and industrial or transport packaging
    C. Packaging has little influence on customer buying decisions.
    D. Packaging can be a major cost in the supply chain.

25. Among the many financial or nonfinancial metrics an organization may have, those associated with critical success factors are labeled as KPIs. What does "KPI" mean?

    A. Key personnel index
    B. Key productivity index
    C. Key performance indicator
    D. Kraft person's invention

26. The finance department has three critical functions. Which of the following is one of those three?

    A. Provide suggestions for new products
    B. Provide support for business and operational planning
    C. Negotiate with suppliers or customers
    D. Buy materials needed for production

27. Which of the following are both carriers and forwarders? (They often have their own aircraft and trucking operations.)

    A. Segregators
    B. Mergers
    C. Integrators
    D. Truckers

28. Which one of the following statements is true about the finance function?

    A. Finance usually incorporates both financial management and accounting services.
    B. Finance is responsible only for financial management services.
    C. Finance rarely incorporates both financial management and accounting services.
    D. Financial management and accounting services are always separate departments.

29. Which one of the following statements is *not* true?

    A. Supply chains for services are different from those for manufacturing.
    B. The concepts of supply chain management can be applied to a service firm's resource and materials requirements.
    C. Services require inputs from the customers that received them.
    D. Service providers are always commercial firms.

30. Which one of the following would be a characteristic of a "continuous flow" operation?

A. Companies that make numerous unique parts or products for many customers
B. Companies that produces high volumes of the same product
C. Companies that produce individual outcomes with distinct and flexible processes
D. Companies that produce a limited number of variations in their products but do so continuously and in high volumes

31. Which one of the following is most often *not* considered part of an organization's logistics function?

A. Transportation
B. Warehousing
C. Human resource management
D. Order fulfillment

32. Metrics must be tied back to strategy. Which one of the following statements is *not* a good reason for doing that?

A. Focusing on measures not tied to strategy is self-defeating.
B. "What gets measured gets attention."
C. Focusing the attention on factors which have no strategic impact is a waste of resources.
D. It makes it easier to terminate employees.

33. Manufacturers have both inbound and outbound flows of materials and products. Which one of the following statements is *not* true regarding those flows?

A. The number of inbound and outbound flows varies considerably among types of manufacturers.
B. A food products or consumer goods producer may have many more outbound shipments than inbound shipments.
C. Inbound shipments always come from customers.
D. Firms that produce automobiles or large appliances have many, many inbound shipments from suppliers.

34. The choice of mode is a trade-off among many factors: cost, timeliness, accessibility, reliability, safety, and security. Regarding the mode of transportation, which one of the following statements is incorrect?

A. In terms of cost, pipelines, water, and rail are least expensive in that order.
B. Using over-the-road transportation is more costly but is much more flexible and faster than pipelines, water, or rail.
C. Airfreight is the most costly transportation mode so products are almost never shipped by air.
D. Large household appliances are most likely to be shipped by rail, truck, or intermodal transportation.

35. Which one of the following specifications identifies what is to be done or what is to be accomplished rather than providing the details of how it is to be achieved?

   A. Performance specifications
   E. Commercial standards
   F. Brand name
   G. Technical specifications

36. There are eight essential steps in the supplier selection process. Which one of the following is first?

   A. Negotiating a contract
   B. Listing the supplier in the accounting database
   C. Development of a supply management strategy
   D. Checking with the legal department about the supplier

37. There are many reasons why a firm may want to go outside for the manufacture of products or for service providers. These reasons include which one of the following?

   A. Lack of in-house expertise to do or create what is needed
   B. To reduce risk by shifting it to a supplier with better capabilities
   C. There is only a sole source capable of providing a product or service
   D. All of the above

38. With regard to the concept of a "value chain," how is value to be added?

   A. By the efficiency and effectiveness of the processes
   B. By the active participation of supply chain members
   C. By focusing close attention on customers
   D. All of these

39. The term that typically refers to the process by which a firm identifies and selects suppliers is _____

   A. NPD.
   B. sourcing.
   C. quoting.
   D. supply chain management.

40. Different types of relationships require different SRM methods. What type of relationship offers the greatest benefits?

   A. A long-term contract for office supplies
   B. Any outsourcing relationship
   C. Short-term relationships that emphasize price
   D. Strategic alliances set up with key or critical suppliers

41. What is the objective of SRM efforts?

   A. Supplier price concessions
   B. Better buyer performance incentives
   C. Mutual long-term value, not short-term price concessions
   D. Reduction in P.O. processing time

42. **When is hard bargaining for a one-time advantage in a single purchase a suitable practice?**
    A. When trying to foster a collaborative relationship
    B. Whenever a low price is desired
    C. When negotiating with key suppliers
    D. When at a flea market

43. **Which of the following statements is *not* true?**
    A. Manufacturing's basic function is to make something.
    B. Firms engaged in manufacturing are called manufacturers.
    C. Retail stores can be either producers or manufacturers.
    D. Mining companies are referred to as producers.

44. **Collaborative governance of the supply chain means:**
    A. There are many individual firms in a supply chain who must work together.
    B. Firms must work closely with local governments.
    C. Retail firms create rules in collaboration with customers.
    D. All the members of the supply chain must team up for social events.

45. **In a market where the buyer is a relatively smaller player, suppliers are not always motivated to reach an agreement. Why?**
    A. The value of the amount of business offered isn't worth the supplier's effort.
    B. The buyer may be a tough negotiator.
    C. It would be an antitrust violation.
    D. It would increase the supplier's taxes.

46. **Negotiators can discuss many issues. How can issues be defined?**
    A. Issues are anything about which there may be at least the appearance of conflict between the parties.
    B. Issues are the same as the "bottom line."
    C. Issues are usually the same outcome the parties want.
    D. Issues reflect the type of personal behaviors in which the negotiators engage.

47. **The concept of total cost of ownership (TCO) is defined as _____**
    A. all purchasing administrative costs combined.
    B. the sum of all costs associated with acquisition, use, ownership, and disposal of any organizational purchase.
    C. the difference between price and cost.
    D. the costs of locating a supplier.

48. **It is supply management's responsibility to understand basic U.S. commercial contract law. What is that set of statutes called?**
    A. Article 2 of the Uniform Commercial Code
    B. United Nations Convention on Contracts for the International Sale of Goods (CISG)

C. The Constitution

D. The Buyer's Bill of Rights

49. It is supply management's responsibility to understand basic international contract law. What is the primary legal resource for that law?

A. United Nations Convention on Contracts for the International Sale of Goods (CISG)

B. The EU Convention on Contracts

C. The UN By-laws

D. The UN Uniform Commercialized Code

50. Which one of the following specifications identifies the details of the design, the materials, and the method of manufacture to be used in creating a product?

A. Performance specifications

B. Commercial standards

C. Brand name

D. Technical specifications

51. Which one of the following is a key cost containment idea that a buyer thinks about regarding specifications?

A. Remember the final customer whenever it is convenient.

B. Always keep the consumer in mind, and judge everything based upon what their perception of value will be.

C. Use unique specifications whenever possible because custom goods always cost less.

D. Seldom use commercial standards because they are more costly.

52. Supply management professionals can play key roles in the NPD process. Which of the following is one?

A. Issue P.O.s quickly.

B. Demand low prices from suppliers.

C. Coordinate with multiple suppliers when their capabilities are needed.

D. Withhold information they do not think is valuable.

53. A negotiation-process-related activity includes setting ground rules. Which one of the following is *not* among them?

A. Participants: who they will be internally and externally

B. Negotiating principles: the style of negotiation to be used

C. Agenda: what issues will be important to the discussions

D. Pricing: setting the limits up front.

54. In the agricultural industry, farmers are producers. Why are they called "producers"?

A. They transform food.

B. They grow crops and raise animals but they don't manufacture them.

C. They are in the market for products.

D. They create cows and milk.

55. When is it best to consider the supply chain's design?
    A. Once it's in place so it can be evaluated
    B. Whenever there is a crisis
    C. Right in the beginning when the products or services are being developed
    D. At the beginning of every week to stay on top of things

56. What type of operation is used to construct a building, create an advertising campaign, or produce any special type of outcome?
    A. Project
    B. Process
    C. Discrete
    D. Ongoing

57. Regarding supplier relationships, a strategic focus is preferable. Why?
    A. A strategic focus is long-term oriented and cost driven.
    B. A tactical focus is long-term oriented and price driven.
    C. It is easier to do.
    D. A strategic focus puts the emphasis on price.

58. When Henry Ford used a method that moved materials from the unloading dock directly to the manufacturing floor he was engaged in a process similar to one used today. What is that process?
    A. JIC
    B. PTO
    C. FYI
    D. JIT

59. Whenever there is no performance, safety, or customer preference that mandates a unique part, which one of the following "design for supply chain" methods should be considered?
    A. Integration
    B. Commonality
    C. Custom design
    D. Customer focus groups

60. Which one of the following statements is considered correct?
    A. Creating a logistics structure that satisfies an "average" customer is always best.
    B. A logistics strategy that is designed to meet the needs of the toughest customers is always best.
    C. A logistics strategy that is designed to meet specific customer segments is best.
    D. Creating a logistics structure that can be changed weekly is best.

61. When retailers take incoming items and move them directly into trucks for outbound delivery to stores, what are they engaged in doing?
    A. Cross-training
    B. Product flow control

C. Single point of destination shipping
D. Cross docking

62. Firms that produce automobiles or large appliances have many, many inbound shipments from suppliers. The number of outbound shipments they have is____ than the inbound.
   A. more
   B. fewer
   C. much more frequent
   D. likely to be lighter

63. The purchase of supplies is known as either a direct or an indirect expenditure. Which one of the following is typically *not* an example of a direct spend item?
   A. Raw materials
   B. Office supplies
   C. Parts and subassemblies
   D. Milk for cheese

64. What is one advantage of a private fleet for some large companies?
   A. It is less expensive.
   B. The trucks carry advertising.
   C. It allows greater flexibility and direct control over costs and lead times
   D. The number of vehicles produces volume-pricing opportunities

65. What transport method carries the bulk of the freight moved in the United States?
   A. Water craft
   B. Class I railroads
   C. Aircraft
   D. Class "C" railroads

66. The amount of inventory held is actually a result of many decisions made in collaboration with other organizational functions. Therefore, which one of the following statements is correct?
   A. Inventory is directly controlled by inventory control personnel.
   B. Inventory is not independently determined by inventory control personnel.
   C. Only finished goods inventory is controlled by inventory control personnel.
   D. Inventory control has no responsibility for what is in stock.

67. One constraint in CSR efforts is the cost associated with it. Why?
   A. Companies that use sustainable production practices must still compete with those which do not.
   B. Companies can always minimize the costs of "going green."
   C. Consumers will always pay the extra costs if they know about them.
   D. The costs to advertise CSR are too great.

68. For shipments within the United States, if an order is shipped "F.O.B" destination, who has the responsibility for it while it is in transit?
    A. Seller
    B. Buyer
    C. Government
    D. Transporter's company

69. What is the metric used to refer to the process by which a customer's order has been received, processed, prepared, and delivered?
    A. Order fulfillment
    B. Order completeness index
    C. Customer satisfaction
    D. Order process cycle

70. What kind of risk is it when we have no choice and no control over an event itself, but we can try to minimize the negative effects?
    A. Unvoluntary
    B. Major
    C. Minor
    D. Involuntary

71. Metrics allow managers "to evaluate and control the performance of the resources for which they are responsible." Why is this important?
    A. This helps focus resources on what will maintain a competitive advantage over the competition.
    B. Different KPIs for different goals are set for everyone.
    C. It will not affect suppliers.
    D. Customers will be more satisfied.

72. What is the notion that businesses have obligations beyond creating products and providing services that generate profit for their owners?
    A. An unsupportable idea
    B. Not an idea many people accept
    C. The basic reason for business to exist
    D. The philosophy behind "corporate social responsibility"

73. Regarding internal supply chain members, the size of an organization and the industry sector in which it operates are major factors in determining who the internal players are.
    A. True
    B. False
    C. Maybe
    D. Never

74. When auto manufacturers create a basic platform on which several models are made, they are using what type of design for the supply chain method?

 A. Modularity
 B. Singularity
 C. Unique design
 D. Random value

75. How are "ethical responsibilities" in CSR defined?

 A. Ethics are societal norms regarding what is fair and reasonable.
 B. They are the laws enacted by a government.
 C. Anything that is legal is right.
 D. Ethics is whatever anybody thinks it is in CSR.

Answers to Quizzes and Final Exam

Chapter 1
1. B
2. A
3. A
4. B
5. A
6. A
7. D
8. C
9. A
10. C
11. B
12. B
13. B
14. A
15. B

Chapter 2
1. A
2. B
3. B
4. B
5. C
6. D
7. B
8. D
9. B
10. C
11. A
12. A
13. C
14. B
15. C

Chapter 3
1. C
2. C
3. A
4. B
5. C
6. C
7. B
8. D
9. A
10. A
11. C
12. A
13. C
14. C
15. C

Chapter 4
1. A
2. C
3. B
4. D
5. C
6. B
7. D
8. B
9. B
10. A
11. A
12. D
13. B
14. B
15. D

Chapter 5
1. B
2. A
3. C
4. B
5. C
6. D
7. D
8. A
9. D
10. B
11. D
12. C
13. A
14. C
15. A

Chapter 6
1. C
2. D
3. C
4. C
5. D
6. B
7. A
8. D
9. A
10. C
11. C
12. D
13. B
14. A
15. D

Chapter 7
1. A
2. B
3. D
4. D
5. C
6. B
7. A
8. B
9. D
10. B
11. C
12. B
13. C
14. B
15. A

Chapter 8
1. C
2. B

3. D
4. A
5. C
6. D
7. B
8. D
9. C
10. B

Chapter 9
1. A
2. C
3. B
4. B
5. D
6. B
7. D
8. A
9. C
10. C
11. D
12. C
13. B
14. A
15. B

Chapter 10
1. B
2. C
3. A
4. D
5. A

Final Exam
1. C
2. B
3. B

4. D
5. C
6. D
7. B
8. A
9. D
10. C
11. C
12. A
13. C
14. A
15. B
16. B
17. D
18. B
19. A
20. D
21. D
22. A
23. A
24. C
25. D
26. B
27. C
28. A
29. D
30. B
31. C
32. D
33. C
34. C
35. A
36. C
37. D
38. D
39. B

40. D
41. C
42. D
43. C
44. A
45. A
46. A
47. B
48. A
49. A
50. D
51. B
52. C
53. D
54. B
55. C
56. A
57. A
58. D
59. B
60. C
61. D
62. B
63. B
64. C
65. B
66. B
67. A
68. A
69. A
70. D
71. A
72. D
73. A
74. A
75. A

Additional Case Studies

Included in this Appendix are additional case studies for Chapters 3, 4, 6, and 8.

Chapter 3 Additional Case Studies

Adaptation Is a Survival Strategy

Dell Incorporated, a leading manufacturer of computers, was an all-star celebrity in supply chain management during the 1990s. While other computer hardware firms were using traditional distribution strategies, Dell chose to sell directly to customers. Instead of make-to-stock, Dell was a make-to-order manufacturer. The supply chain efficiencies Dell achieved became legendary, and their practices widely imitated. Other companies wanted to benefit from lean supply chains that could reduce inventory and bring lead times from weeks to days.

But that was the 1990s. In the decades since then, the market, the electronic devices, and consumer requirements have changed dramatically. The greatest opportunity for growth in the computer hardware market is now in developing economies, where the public transport infrastructure is lacking. That makes it tough to get products into customers' hands. Devices, such as smart phones and small tablet computers, are also stripping away PC sales in more mature markets. Customers no longer expect to be tied to a desktop in order to work, communicate, or play with the applications that computer technology offers.

Customer-focused supply chain initiatives and high-performance command centers are part of a plan to reinvigorate the company. The supply chain focus is at the customer end, and activities in the chain are continuously adjusted to meet those customers' needs. The command centers constantly monitor supply chain activities and allow the company to react quickly to changes or disruptions. This keeps customer service levels and customer loyalty high.

Change is the nature of the universe and the enemy of inflexible strategies. Every strategy can fail unless it adapts to a changing environment.

Extending the Brand from Beer to Glasses

Brewer's today are challenged to come up with strategies for competing in a crowded market with flat sales growth. The Boston Beer Company is no exception. The brewer of the Sam Adams brand chose to extend its product line to include a distinctive glass that would differentiate its beer.

The idea was to accentuate the taste and aroma of their products rather than create new recipes. To do that, the new product development team explored the idea of a new glass! Through customer research and a bit of science, the team came up with a new design for a special Sam Adams beer glass. Boston Beer is convinced that this new glass helps differentiate their products. The shape of the glass, its rim, and its thinner walls were specifically designed to enhance the effects on the beer drinker's senses.

The new glass is now a popular product in its own right, but it took a serious collaborative effort among both internal and external supply chain members to make it happen. Inside Boston Beer, understanding the customers and the market, executing a process for product development, validating the design, and creating a distribution plan, all required collaboration among marketing, supply management, finance, production (brewing), logistics, and information technology (IT).

Agile Postponement

There is an old saying in manufacturing, "At least you can be sure of one thing about forecasts—they're always wrong." The further into the future the plan, the more likely it is to be inaccurate. There are a couple of things that help cause that inaccuracy. First, it's hard to be sure about the future until it gets here. The number of variables at play in the business environment is huge. Secondly, while estimates of the aggregate demand for a product family might be pretty close, trying to judge exactly what model, color, and price customers will want is challenging. Of course, there are some products with fairly stable, predicable demand patterns, such as grocery staples (bread, eggs, milk, etc.). In other product categories, such as apparel and consumer electronics, things aren't so easy.

But what if you could wait until "the last minute" to configure your product to meet whatever the customers wanted? That is, what if you could "postpone" adding a product attribute, such as the color of clothing or the size of a harddrive, until you were more certain what the customer wanted? That's what some firms are doing.

Postponement is a good example of how business strategy initiates supply chain strategy. Michael Dell decided to give customers what they wanted, when they wanted it. The Dell direct-to-customer model drove the need for a supply chain designed to meet it. Zara in apparel has been the poster child for fast reaction to changing demand. By tightly controlling the upstream and downstream supply chain, Zara is able to rapidly change styles, colors, and product mix.

Not every product is a candidate for postponement. But innovative ones that have short life cycles or a large variety of options, or are subject to the whims of fashion are certainly good choices.

Chapter 4 Additional Case Studies

Conflict Minerals and the Law

Resource availability is a major issue for some manufacturers and producers. Geography, geology, and climate are the factors that influence where materials are sourced. For example, coffee, cocoa for chocolate, and hops for beer are dependent upon geography and climate; geology determines where the rareearth metals used in high tech electronics can be found.

In 2014, resource availability will be impacted by another factor—U.S. law. In May of 2014, companies will need to comply with the U.S. Securities and Exchange Commission's (SEC) "Conflict Minerals Rule." The rule is required by the Dodd-Frank Act and is intended to prevent armed groups from making money on the sale of tantalum, tin, tungsten, and gold.

The rule will require companies to disclose whether or not their products contain any of these four minerals. If they do contain those minerals, they must also disclose whether or not those minerals came from countries covered by the law. This will be a challenge, since compliance with the law will require going way upstream in the supply chain to third or fourth tier suppliers. Supply management personnel are at the center of efforts to create policies and procedures to work with their suppliers and meet this legal requirement.

In Make or Buy Decisions, Soft Costs Sometimes Tip the Balance

The choice to make or buy is a decision not often faced by distributors. The usual wisdom is that a company should stick with their core competency and contract outside for anything else. A few years ago, a major U.S. distribution company was faced with just such a tough decision. They had been offering a branded version of a basic two-shelf plastic utility cart for a number of years, and it was selling well. So when the manufacturer announced they were going to discontinue the basic cart and redesign it, the distributor's product management team was concerned that the manufacturer might be "fixing something that wasn't broken."

At the same time that the cart manufacturer made its announcement, a number of distribution companies began launching their own "private label" versions of the basic cart. That's when the real story emerged. The manufacturer's patents had run out, and low-cost competitors had moved into their profitable product space. To counter the introduction of the low-cost knockoffs, the manufacturer had decided to discontinue their more commoditized product and go up market with a higher-value-added cart.

This left the distribution company with a lot to consider: do they continue with a one brand strategy and simply go along with the manufacturer's change, or go after market share in the "private label" segment of the market? Research showed many of their competitors were sourcing their low-cost version of the cart from manufacturers in China. This is a common strategy in the market for material-handling products. If they were to pursue a private label line, the distributor would need to purchase expensive molds and find a manufacturer with the capabilities to produce the product.

After gathering all of the data on the different options, the distributor was ready to make a decision; however, the answer was not clear cut. Looking just at the numbers, buying tooling and producing the product in Asia seemed like a good low-cost option, providing them the margin to compete. Yet, there were some major concerns about the soft costs associated with long lead times, an untested supplier, and the fact that they would be entering into a contract manufacturing agreement with an international supplier, something that was not a core competency for the distribution company. That left two additional options: continue the one brand strategy, or try to get a low-cost cart produced in the United States.

Ultimately the decision was made to have the cart produced in the United States. Because most of the production could be automated, the cost was low enough to allow the distribution company to price the product competitively. The product was a success, and as demand rose, the shorter lead time from the manufacturer became a key factor in keeping the product in stock and fulfilling orders.

Honda: "Tough but Fair"

Over many years, the author has had an opportunity to speak with numerous Honda suppliers. In every discussion about what Honda was like as a customer, they all had the same comment, "Tough but very fair." In June 2013, *Automotive News* published the results of a poll that appeared to confirm that perspective. In the article, "Poll: Honda most often eases material costs," David Sedgwick wrote:

> *If you're a supplier and you're worried about fluctuating costs of your raw materials, Honda, Ford, Toyota and Nissan are the best customers to deal with. According to a survey of 88 suppliers published last week by IRN Inc., Honda Motor Co. is most likely to offset raw material price increases. For example, 79 percent of suppliers said Honda was more likely or somewhat likely to offset price increases in a satisfactory manner, while only 16 percent said it was least likely or somewhat unlikely to do so.*

Source: David Sedgwick, "Poll: Honda most often eases material costs", *Automotive News*, June 10, 2013, 12:01 am EST, http://www.autonews.com.

Chapter 6 Additional Case Study

Even Giants Have Inventory Headaches

In March of 2012, Bloomberg.com ran a story about Wal-Mart's "inventory problems." The news service reported that Wal-Mart expected to increase profit by seeing to it that their shelves were well stocked. That benefit was to come from a projected $5 billion increase in sales. These were sales that were being lost to out-of-stock situations.

Unfortunately, almost one year later in February of 2013, Bloomberg again ran a story on Wal-Mart's continuing inventory problems, "Wal-Mart Struggles to Restock Store Shelves as U.S. Sales Slump." Little information has been disclosed by the company. There is speculation that Wal-Mart's centralized distribution may cause longer lead times in replenishing store stocks. Whatever the reasons, the importance of managing inventory isn't lost on the retail industry. If supply chain snags can cause inventory headaches for giants like Wal-Mart, any company could be vulnerable.

Source: http://www.bloomberg.com/news/2013-02-27/wal-mart-s-slowness-stock-shelves-worsens-as-sales-stay-s.html.

Chapter 8 Additional Case Study

Supply Chain Technology Helped Put Wal-Mart on Top

Wal-Mart is the giant among retailers. In fact, in terms of sales and revenue, Wal-Mart is the largest company of any kind in the world. According to its 2012 annual report, "Today Wal-Mart operates more than 10,000 retail units under 69 different banners in 27 countries." Last year, "Net sales increased by 5.9 percent to $443.9 billion, and consolidated operating income grew by 4 percent to $26.6 billion."

Wal-Mart's supply chain network and systems are frequently acknowledged as a major factor in the company's growth and success. The backbone of that supply chain network is information technology. In his 1992 book, *Made in America*, the company's founder, Sam Walton, wrote: "Truthfully, I never viewed computers as anything more than necessary overhead." In spite of that perspective, Wal-Mart was an early and aggressive adopter of IT innovations.

Since 1975 Wal-Mart has actively embraced technology to manage its business and inventories, record point-of-sale data, and communicate with suppliers. During the 1980s, the company introduced barcode scanners and built the largest private satellite network of its time.

Wal-Mart's progress in applying IT to the supply chain has been continuous but not without some issues, such as the company's RFID initiatives, which have yet to be completed. It's also true that retailers worldwide have largely caught up to Wal-Mart when it comes to integrating technology into their supply chain operations. But Wal-Mart's lead in maximizing IT to its strategic advantage still persists.

Suggested Additional Reading and Information Resources

Textbooks

Bowersox, Donald, Closs, David, and Cooper, M. Bixby, *Supply Chain Logistics Management*. New York: McGraw-Hill, 2012.

Chopra, Sunil and Meindl, Peter, *Supply Chain Management*, 5th ed. Upper Saddle River, NJ: Prentice Hall, 2013.

Jacobs, F. Robert and Chase, Richard, *Operations and Supply Chain Management*, 14th ed. New York: McGraw-Hill, 2013.

Professional Trade Books

Burt, David, Petcavage, Sheila, and Pinkerton, Richard, *Proactive Purchasing in the Supply Chain: The Key to World-Class Procurement*. New York: McGraw-Hill, 2011.

Cohen, Shoshanah and Roussel, Joseph, *Strategic Supply Chain Management: The Five Disciplines for Top Performance*, 2nd ed. New York: McGraw-Hill, 2013.

Internet Information Resources[*]

Associations Websites

APICS—http://www.apics.org/

APICS is a professional association for supply chain and operations management.

CAPS Research—http://www.capsresearch.org/

CAPS Research is a nonprofit supply chain research organization jointly sponsored by the W. P. Carey School of Business at Arizona State University and the Institute for Supply Management.

Chartered Institute of Purchasing and Supply (CIPS)—http://www.cips.org/

CIPS is a professional association for those engaged in purchasing and supply chain management.

Council of Supply Chain Management Professionals (CSCMP)—http://cscmp .org/

CSCMP is a professional association for SCM professionals.

Institute for Supply Management (ISM)—http://www.ism.ws/membership/ content.cfm?ItemNumber=4733

ISM is a professional association for individuals in the supply management field.

International Federation of Purchasing and Supply Management (IFPSM)— http://www.ifpsm.org/

IFPSM is the union of 48 worldwide purchasing associations.

National Association of State Procurement Officials (NASPO)—http://www .naspo.org/

NASPO is a nonprofit association whose membership includes the directors of the central purchasing offices in each of the 50 states, the District of Columbia, and the territories of the United States.

Supply Chain Management Association (SCMA) British Columbia—http:// www.scmabc.ca/

The SCMA BC is part of the Supply Chain Management Association (SCMA), an association in Canada for supply chain management professionals.

[*] *This list is not all-inclusive. Many additional resources can be located with Internet search engines.*

Online Publications

Supply & Demand Chain Executive—http://www.sdcexec.com/
A magazine that covers the entire global supply chain.

SupplyChainBrain—http://www.supplychainbrain.com
SupplyChainBrain is a supply chain management information resource.

Supply Chain Digest—http://www.scdigest.com/
Supply Chain Digest is a weekly online newsletter for supply chain and logistics.

Supply Management—http://www.supplymanagement.com/
Supply Management magazine is a monthly publication for procurement and supply chain professionals published on behalf of the Chartered Institute of Purchasing & Supply.

Index

O

P

WITHDRAWN

CPSIA information can be obtained
at www.ICGtesting.com
Printed in the USA
FFOW04n2108170418
46293361-47781FF